CALLED TO BE
CHRISTIAN

CALLED TO BE CHRISTIAN

by Philip R. Hoh

Terence Y. Mullins, editor
Roland Shutts, artist

MUHLENBERG PRESS
PHILADELPHIA

Copyright, 1961, by
THE MUHLENBERG PRESS
Printed in U.S.A.

Second Printing

Published under the auspices of the
Boards of Parish Education of
The American Evangelical Lutheran Church
The Augustana Lutheran Church
The Finnish Evangelical Lutheran Church
The United Lutheran Church in America

COMMENTS FOR THE READER

This book deals with the most important things in your life: you, people, and God. It does not merely present facts to learn or some ideas the church considers important, but it is meant to bring you face to face with a way of life.

Parts of this book will need careful and repeated reading. The book is written to stimulate your thinking. It raises some questions for which no one yet has found an answer. And it tells truths that no one can ignore.

Some of the words used may be new to you. They are used because there are no other words which do the job as well as they do. In every area of life — in sports, hobbies, medicine, business — special words are needed. The church has some, too. You can't talk clearly about your religion without them.

In the margins are numbers. They refer you to the two indexes in the back of the book. Numbers with an asterisk have Bible passage and hymns listed in *Index II.* By looking these up in your Bible or in the *Service Book and Hymnal,* you can see how our Christian faith grows out of what God has said through Bible writers, and how our hymns put these thoughts into poetry for worship.

As you are reading this book, there are three questions you will constantly need to ask yourself.

1. Does this apply to me?
2. If it does, do I want to follow it?
3. If I do, how will my life be changed?

This book, because it deals with the whole Christian faith, is important reading for you. It is meant to be fun, too. Study it. Enjoy it. Learn what God says about you, about other people, and about himself.

I

GOD AND MAN

YOUR LIMITATIONS

There are people in the world who are stronger than you, who are smarter than you, who are handsomer or prettier. No matter how hard you try, you will never be quite as strong or quite as smart or quite as good looking as they are.

You have your limitations — lots of them. We all do. This is 1°
part of being a human. Some people are better at one thing than others. That's life. We accept this.

The five-year-old girl accepts the fact that she is not as tall as her fourteen-year-old brother (we hope!). Your parents will always be older than you. You can't do a thing about it.

There are some things none of us can do. We can't be in two different places at the same time. We can't start out with absolutely nothing and make something out of it (except in arguments). We don't know how to make a dead object into a live one. We can't live without food. And so on. All this is part of being human. We have to accept it. We human beings are limited in many, many ways. God is not. We are in a cage, he isn't. Look at four of the many ways we are caged and God isn't.

1. Intellectual Limitations

Think of the activity that goes on in your back yard (if you 2°
have one). The grass is growing, each blade has thousands of cells, some turning sunlight into energy, others rapidly replacing dead cells so that the blade will grow. There are ants working at their various jobs. Other insects are working, playing, surviving, and dying. Little fungi are turning dead leaves into material that the plant roots can absorb, etc., etc., etc. Millions and millions of things are going on in every square foot of the yard — all organized, balanced, all with beauty, with purpose.

You could work all your life and not be able to organize even one little section of your yard. But God created heaven and earth, our solar system, thousands of solar systems, the universe, and who knows what else. He created all this and planned it down to the last detail, to the infinitesimal particle that makes up the structure of an atom's proton — or something so small we don't know whether it is matter or energy or space or what. What a mind God must have!

For thousands of years people have worked to learn more and more about the universe. They passed their knowledge on to others. Civilizations grew up. They had their scientists, educators, politicians, workers in all areas. They passed on what they had learned. Finally the sum total of human knowledge comes down to your generation. Today *you* have available the total knowledge of all mankind, the wisdom of billions of people over hundred thousands of years. Put it all together. Collect all the talents of every living person. Now — can you make one leaf? Can you start with oxygen and hydrogen and carbon and whatever elements you can lay your hands on and put together one living leaf? No. But God arranges this earth so that trillions of leaves come out every year. What kind of mind, what wisdom God must have!

Care to match wits with God? Some people try. It's not that God is a little smarter than we humans are; God is completely smarter. The thinking we can do is never going to be able to figure out all that God planned. We've made a lot of progress — rockets and atomic research, vaccines, and such things. We still can't make one leaf.

The point is that we are intellectually limited. Our math works according to certain rules we've set it in ($2 + 2 = 4$). We can't think any other way. We think of truth as some sort of mathematical and scientific thing. It may be; it may not be. God knows. We don't. Final truth may be a lot different from what we humans think it is. When Jesus said, "I am the way, the truth, and the life," by *truth* he wasn't referring to the idea that $2 + 2 = 4$, or that you need food to live, or that things expand

8

when they get hot (except ice). Jesus was thinking of truth much more important than these trivial bits of scientific information.

What is truth? Pontius Pilate asked that question when Jesus was brought before him. He decided he didn't know the answer. His actions proved it. Great human thinkers have been worrying about truth for a long time. One poet said that truth is beauty, which is a nice idea except that we can't agree what beauty is. (The fact that he said so doesn't make it true, anyhow.) Probably only God knows what truth really is. We're talking about truth, not things that are very probable on earth, which is what usually passes for truth. (You will find the word "probable" used many times in this book.) 5*

Possibly there is only one way in which you can be sure of knowing what is true. Have all the facts, or have someone who knows all the facts tell you. But only God has the mind to know all the facts, so if we are to know the truth, he will have to tell us what it is. 6*

2. Spacial Limitations

We are also limited by living in bodies which have three dimensions. All things have length and breadth and height. The paper this is printed on has length and width and some thickness. If it had no thickness there would be no paper. Ideas and emotions like love or pain may not take up space, but they are connected with things that do; an emotion doesn't float about without somebody to emote it. 7

We live in a certain kind of space. If any other kind exists, we have no way of knowing it. Maybe there is some kind of space with another dimension. Maybe our kind has other qualities which we aren't built to experience. God is not limited as we are. He can act freely where we are blocked. 8*

Does space have any end? If you took a rocket ship into the universe, would you come to the end of space? No matter how far you traveled, there would always be more space, but it is impossible to go through all the space there is. Better space ships won't solve the problem. We're in a cage.

9   God is not limited by space. He planned and created it. He's bigger than it is. He controls it. How "big" must God be to be able to create our sun — or a million suns. And what if this universe turns out to be a little speck in something greater!

3. Temporal Limitations

10*   We think in terms of time. Suppose you were suddenly in a world where absolutely nothing moved. Now, what time is it? How could you find an answer? Time is the way we measure the rate at which things change. Our system of minutes and hours is an arbitrary system by which we measure other movements. If something doesn't change, it doesn't age. It is unaffected by time.

11   If God doesn't change, does this mean that he is not involved with time? If he doesn't change, does this mean that he can't move? Confusing, isn't it?

Remember how long a day was when you were young? The older you get the shorter the days are. Some days seem longer than others. A few seconds of pain seem endless compared to a few seconds of pleasure. How long did the dream take in which you lived a whole day's events? How long is time? Is it what the clock says, or the way you feel it flies or drags or passes?

12*   Suppose you could get rid of time, then what would life be like? Would there be beginnings and endings? Would things last, or just be? Who knows? Only God. He goes beyond time; it doesn't limit him. We're caged; he isn't.

4. Limitations in Righteousness

13   None of us is perfect. We're not even sure what *perfect* is. We can recognize our faults (maybe) and imagine what we'd be like without them. This would then be perfection. But this assumes we know what *faults* are.

Some kinds of perfection we can figure out, if we carefully limit the ingredients to a few we can handle. Add up a column of simple figures. Add it up right and you have a perfect answer. Draw a circle. If it has no kinks in it, then it's a perfect circle. Well, almost! Nobody has ever drawn a really perfect circle. A

10

compass helps, but magnify the circle enough and you will see flaws. But we can imagine a perfect circle — almost.

What is a perfect tree? How many leaves, how thick a trunk, how long a life? Can a tree be perfect, or can it only be a tree?

What is a perfect person? You might say that a perfect person 14 makes no mistakes. But what is a mistake? And who decides what is a mistake? Only a perfect person could be sure, because a person who makes mistakes might make a mistake about what a mistake is. So who knows what a perfect person is? Only God. 15 For Christians then, sin is only fully known in God's eyes. We are merely good enough to know that none of us is perfect. We rarely live up to our own standards, and never to God's.

Since none of us is perfect, we spend most of our lives playing around with a lesser idea, trying to figure out what is good and what is better. Our lives are spent placing values on things. "Will 16 I be better off if I ask mother or if I ask father? Is it better to get a good grade in Latin or watch an extra TV show? Should I be a teacher at a lower salary or an engineer at a higher one? How much should I give to the church? Is it worth while riding with the gang in Bill's car if Bill is a reckless driver? Which is more important to me, God or me?"

We place values on everything. Are they the right values? Who knows? Only God, because only he sees all the connections, 17* all the relationships, all the outcomes, all the motives, all the possibilities. We're in the valleys; he's on the mountain top. We're caged; he's not. We see everything from our own personal slant, and it is a slant. We humans aren't perfect, sinless, righteous. Only God is.

Summary

We are limited. God isn't. Why is this important to remember? 18* For one thing, it reminds us that God is much greater than we are. Iu fact, he isn't just much greater; he's completely greater, greater in every way. Where we see one jigsaw puzzle piece, he sees the whole picture. He doesn't need to be limited by anything we can do. He's so tremendous that we can't even imagine how tremendous he is.

Christianity is concerned about God and our relationship to him. When we humans try to guess what God is like, we are obviously going to be way off base much of the time. But if God somehow tells us what he is like and what he wants, we'll be 19* better off. Yet even then we will not be able fully to understand him.

Suppose a girl tries to tell a boy what it is like to be a girl. Some things he will understand. About other things he may only get a vague idea. He's never been a girl; how can he fully understand? How can a dog understand what it is to be a man? How can man understand what it is to be God? All through our study we will be dealing with things which are beyond us. There will be many questions for which we have no answers. Yet, when we remember that God is not limited, we Christians can relax, because we know that he knows. When your doctor prescribes a pill, you don't usually know what's in it, or all the reasons why he gave it to you. But if you have faith in him, you take it and are content, because you know he knows. So with us and God.

There are a lot of mysteries in the Christian faith. They reflect our limitations. It is handy to know why mysteries are mysteries — so you can stop worrying about them. You can also save a lot of time spent in useless discussion once you know that something is beyond human ability to understand. (It's positively amazing how much time and energy is wasted by people arguing some religious points nobody can ever solve.)

THE MEETING OF GOD WITH MAN

20* According to the best information we have — and it isn't very complete — when God first caused man to be, man recognized God as his Creator, felt at home with God, enjoyed God's company, wanted to do what God asked him to, was a satisfied being. Man really lived — for a very short time!

But, you remember, God had made humans with minds of their own. For some reason man began to take himself too seri-

12

ously, got a little too proud of himself, and in the process broke off relations with God. This was a fatal mistake. Breaking off relations with the Creator was breaking off relations with the source of life. God knew that though a man might continue to exist a number of years before he died, if he turned his back on God, he was pretty dead already. (Note in the story of the Prodigal Son how Jesus uses the words "dead" and "alive" to refer to the son's relationship with his father — cf. Luke 15:11-32.) 21*

Not wanting this, God tried to win man back, tried to get humans to recognize that he was really the source of life. The most God could do — and still be loving — was to keep himself as near to man as possible and hope that man would respond. But you know how people are. They hate to admit that they owe 22* anything to anybody. They pretend they can take care of themselves. God had a hard time getting people to accept him. He still does.

Meeting God in His Word

If you add up all the ways that God communicates himself to men, all the ways he reveals himself, and everything he "says," 23* this is called the "Word of God." *Word* with a capital W stands for much more than just words that are spoken. It's a special term. (I give you my *word* this is true.) Since the Bible is the greatest source of information about himself that God has revealed to us, we call the Bible the Word of God. Since Jesus is 24* the truth about God put in human form, and comes from God, we call Jesus the Word. When the pastor preaches what God 25 wants said, we say he is preaching the Word. These are the more 26 obvious forms of the Word of God, but any way that God chooses to speak to us is his Word.

Because it is God speaking, not just another human being, this Word has additional meanings. It carries weight. It is the absolute truth — the only absolute truth the world can ever know. 27* It carries its own guarantee that what it says, goes. God stands behind his Word. He doesn't back down or change his mind. We change our minds because we've made mistakes, or were confused, or are scared. None of these things happens to God. When he "gives his Word," that's it!

28° Jeremiah said that God's Word is like a hammer which breaks a rock into pieces. He meant that what God says, happens. The Word of God means a lot of other things, too, but here we are concerned with how he contacts us. He does this by his Word.

If this Word, in any form, can bring us to a right response to God, into a right relationship, we call this contact a "means of
29 grace." By a "means of grace" God gives himself to us. When someone is gracious to you, he is giving something of himself to you, not because you paid him or earned his favor, but because
30° that's the way he is; he is *gracious*. Obviously we can't buy anything from God, although people have tried. (What does God need with which you could pay him? Love, possibly? Even that won't work, because the moment you think in terms of payment and buying, then it isn't love, is it?) So when God does something for us, he is gracious. We receive his gifts by the *grace of God*.

31 We call baptism a means of grace, because through it God helps us, even though we have not earned his help. Holy Communion is another way he helps, a means of grace. God can use other people to reach us. Sometimes he may work through our parents or a friend who has been influenced by his Word. These people, then, become a means of grace. Terms like "the Word of God" and "means of grace" are important because they are part of the language of Christians. With them the Christian can say whole paragraphs of thinking in a few words.

It isn't easy to point out places where God contacts us. He is so different from us that we don't see him with our eyes as we see animals or people. In fact, "No one has ever seen God." (John 1:18). We can't touch him or hear him in the usual way. People sometimes tell us to pray to God and listen for his answer.
32 But our ears don't hear a thing. We are so used to meeting persons through our seeing and hearing and touching that when we can't meet someone this way, we are at a loss.

14

Perhaps this is why we so eagerly grasp those ways in which God does speak to us through our senses, like in reading the Bible or hearing the preacher, or tasting the Communion wine. Maybe that's why God has given us sacraments like Communion, so that there is something we can see and touch and taste which ties in with his presence. Perhaps that's one reason why God sent Jesus, so that at least once in history we could see and hear and touch something of God. 33 34

The way a lot of Bible stories are written they read as though God actually made physical contacts with people. He "walked" in the Garden of Eden with Adam and Eve. Moses on Mount Sinai saw him "face to face." Young Samuel heard his voice. So did Elijah. Paul, on the road to Damascus, saw a vision of Christ. The martyr Stephen "saw the heavens opened and the Son of Man standing at the right hand of God." Besides these startling contacts with God, another type of strong contact is frequently mentioned. 35°

Jacob wrestled with an "angel of the Lord;" Ezekiel saw a vision of the throne of God; Isaiah also saw the Lord in a sort of vision. Elisha's young apprentice saw "the chariots of God." The shepherds witnessed a host of angels in the skies at Bethlehem. Those present at Jesus' baptism observed the Spirit of God descend as a dove does. And when the disciples were together at Pentecost, God's Spirit came on them "like tongues of fire." 36°

Has anything like that ever happened to you? Probably not. Will it ever? Who knows? When we read of these obvious contacts God has made, there are several things to remember. In the Bible we have two thousand years of history. Of the hundreds of thousands of people who lived through those years, some obviously felt closer to God than others. A few were given exceptional insight. Is it really so startling, then, that in all this history a few outstanding people were able to see more clearly than the rest of us? As you study men like Abraham, Moses, Elijah, you see that these men are head and shoulders above the rest of us. If any men could work miracles, it would be these men whom God had chosen to speak for him. And you know, in the whole 37

Old Testament, with a few exceptions, it is only these men who did work miracles.

38   Another thing we have to remember is that these men had to use words to tell of their remarkable experiences with God. They had to use the words which existed in their language. What words are there to describe something that is beyond most human experience? We have the words they chose to use. Sometimes we can only guess what the experience was really like. What, for example, is a "vision?" Until you've had one, how can you know? Have you ever tried, for example, to describe a toothache to a person who never had one? Any luck? Words don't quite do the job, do they?

Some churches make a lot of fuss about startling contacts people may have with God. Some few churches insist that every
39*   member must have some spectacular experience in which he is "converted" to Christianity. He must be able to name the place, the date, even the minute when this occurred. Lutherans are certainly not going to deny that some people have sudden vivid experiences with God, experiences through which a whole life may completely change. A rotten man can become a saint, just like that! It does happen. Praise God when it does. Look what happened to Paul.

But we Lutherans don't expect it to happen to most of us.
40*   We expect to grow in grace — as the confirmation service says. The more normal way for Christians to meet God is to grow increasingly close to him, the way you grow up.

If you used to play with a little girl when you were five or six years old, and now meet her again after many years, you notice quite a change, don't you? It's startling. You probably won't recognize her. She's grown. But if the two of you have been neighbors all the time, and you've seen each other every day, she has grown up just as much, but you didn't take note of any change from day to day. This is the way most Christians grow.

41   We were brought to God by our parents through baptism. Through the years God has worked with us in the ways he chose. Sometimes we may have felt his working, but mostly it was too

16

subtle for us to notice. Hopefully, we have grown through the years. God has been working through Christian teachers, Christian parents, Christian friends, the pastor, and in many other ways. At this moment we are studying more about God. All this should bring us ever closer to him. This is the usual way God works: slowly, steadily, quietly.

A few young people expect something startling to happen to them when they are confirmed and take their first Communion. It rarely does. The importance of being confirmed is that you 42 take on your own shoulders the responsibility of being a Christian. If you have been baptized, your sponsors (parents or others) have had that responsibility. It was their faith that led to your baptism. They asked God to accept you as his child. They promised to bring you up as a Christian. At confirmation you are supposed to be able to do your own thinking and deciding. You study what your church teaches. You decide for yourself whether you accept these ideas, whether you want to be one of Jesus' followers, whether you feel that the Lutheran point of view is most suitable to you. If so, you are confirmed. If not, you aren't.

What is it that changes? The place of responsibility. With confirmation comes all the change you would expect when you have made up your own mind to be a Christian. Nothing more, nothing less. If you have really made up your mind to accept Jesus as your Lord, God is immensely happy and all the saints and angels rejoice. You probably won't see this taking place.

Of course, if a young person is confirmed only because his 43 parents expect him to be and the rest of the class is going to be, then even this important shift of responsibility doesn't take place, and confirmation is meaningless. This is unfortunate, but frequent. God respects the individual who has the honesty not to be confirmed if he isn't ready.

One fine Christian, talking about God's influence on his life, noted that we are conscious of being influenced by other people, by the weather, by parents, by all sorts of things, but rarely do we assume that God has been influencing us. If we get to heaven,

17

says this writer, and can see clearly what really happened during our lives on earth, probably our first statement to God will be,
44* "So it was you all the time." How many times has God steered us, and we have not even suspected it. How many times was our life saved because God stepped in behind the scenes? One hymn writer (Hymn 547, SBH) speaking of the way things seem to go on earth, said:

> "Though the cause of evil prosper,
> Yet 'tis truth alone is strong;
> Though her portion be the scaffold
> And upon the throne be wrong,
> Yet that scaffold sways the future,
> And, behind the dim unknown,
> Standeth God amid the shadow,
> Keeping watch above his own."

45* It's easy to confuse our own interpretation of an event with God's will. It's not easy, for example, to tell whether the shiver that runs down your spine when you hear a certain hymn is due to God or sentiment. Probably we make the mistake of discounting God's work rather than over-emphasizing it. The people who wrote the Bible gave God credit for almost everything that happened. We give him credit for practically nothing. They were more nearly right than we are.

There is no complete set of rules for knowing when God has stepped into the course of events, or which thoughts he has inspired. Lutherans feel strongly that each individual must follow
46* his own conscience. If you believe that God has called you to do something, this you must do. Whether or not this is a true call from God, or is from another source, the Lutheran Church will not decide for you. This does not mean that you are free to rely on your own opinion in every case. There are many points where God has made clear himself and his demands for us. For example, we know that God is holy; that is, he is unalterably opposed to sin. Once you feel that you are right, however, you must stand on that position, come what may. This is your right and your duty.

18

You remember that Luther, standing before the tribunal in the town of Worms, Germany, faced those who were asking him to renounce what he had written, and under threat of death said, "Here I stand. I can do nothing else. God help me." It is a basic Lutheran belief that when an individual believes God has spoken to him, he must act accordingly, even if governments or churches disagree.

But—and there is usually a "but"—the intelligent Christian should have enough sense to check his opinions against the clearest revelation of God that he can find—to be sure that he is not fooling himself or being fooled. (Luther and Paul suggested that the Devil would take the form of an angel if he could win people that way!) The intelligent Christian will prayerfully check what he believes to be God's Word against the teaching of Jesus, which he *knows* is God's Word. If what the Christian thinks God said is contrary to what Jesus taught, then it is false; the Christian has mistaken other ideas for the Word of God. On the other hand, if what the Christian believes to be God's Word seems to be in line with Jesus' teachings, it very well may be God speaking.

A second good check is to compare our beliefs with the tradition of the Christian church. The church is made up of people, and they have been wrong many times. But basically the centers (not the fringes) of Christian thinking are close to Jesus' teachings. God's spirit has helped many fine Christians face problems and make decisions similar to the one being considered. If the message to an individual disagrees with the thinking and acting of the great men of the church, then be careful. It is not likely to be correct. You may have distorted the truth and be remaking God's Word into your own patterns.

So the Christian checks his conscience by the known Word of God, Christ, and by Christian tradition. Even with these procedures there will be many times when the sensitive Christian will not be sure whether God has spoken to him or not. Then he acts according to his best judgment. He follows this up with two other actions.

19

First, he asks God's forgiveness in case his own ideas and
50 feelings have gotten in the way of God's desires. Knowing that
he makes mistakes in many ways, even by "secret thoughts and
desires which I cannot fully understand," (Prayer of Confession
from the Communion Service), he asks God to make up for his
errors and in the future help him hear God's Word more clearly.
Then, if it seems that the decision was a right one, the Christian
51 gives God the credit for it and thanks God for having shown him
what he ought to do. The Christian gives God the credit because
he knows from his own experience, increasingly, that everything
good starts out from God, that God is the source of good, that
his nature is the standard by which we decide what good is.
Furthermore, man's experience shows him, increasingly, that
when left to his own nature he sure can get things fouled up.
So the Christian gives God the credit. "For thine is the kingdom,
the power, and the glory" is one way of saying it.

Every Christian wishes that God would speak to him more
clearly and more often. He wishes that the Bible, and especially
Jesus' teachings, would tell him simply and directly what to do
52 in every situation. Wouldn't it be nice if the Bible were a complete blueprint for all of life, and all we had to do was to follow
it in detail, knowing we were always doing what God wants?

But God doesn't always communicate to us that clearly, and
53* the Bible doesn't always give us the answers to our questions.
Jesus just didn't meet some of the problems we meet. Think
what would happen if everything were that clear. We would
become like machines, following a set of rules. Our only choice
would be to follow or refuse to follow. God has chosen not to set
up life this way. Perhaps it is in the nature of love that it cannot
be fitted into rules. Perhaps it is in the nature of rules that they
are inferior to love.

Anyhow, God communicates his Word to us as he chooses and
as we let him. Those who love God are more aware of him and
his desires than those who don't much care. Our job is to tune
in on all of God's wave lengths, keep the radio plugged in, the
volume turned up, and interference at a minimum. We can be
20

sure that God is busy finding ways to help us be the kind of humans he made us to be—creatures who know and love their Creator.

What Does God Want?

When you talk to people you have a reason for doing so. You want their companionship, or want them to give you something they have, or want to give them something you have. Whatever the reason, you don't talk without having something to say. When God communicates to us, he has something to say. It isn't in the nature of God to be trivial. 54

There are a number of good reasons why we should pay close attention to whatever God wants of us: fear, self-fulfillment, and love. Our English translations of the Bible use the word *fear* quite often in the Old Testament. "The fear of the Lord is the beginning of wisdom," for example. Fear, as the Bible writers used it, combines a number of meanings. Luther, when he wrote his *Small Catechism*, used the word "fear" in most of his explanations of the Ten Commandments. Here, too, we see an interesting combination of meanings in that word. Luther says, "We should so fear and love God as to . . ."—and goes on to say what the commandments tell us we should do. You can see that to Luther fear and love were not opposites which couldn't get along together. How can you love someone you're afraid of? When the Bible and Luther use the word "fear" they are speaking *also* of awe, reverence, respect. God is so tremendous, so powerful, so wise, so loving that we contemplate him in absolute amazement. 55* 56*

If you happen to like a terrific thunderstorm or the surging power of a great waterfall or the majestic persistence of the rolling ocean, then you know in part how love and fear can be combined. There is something magnificent about being a little speck of nature when a large chunk of nature goes wild and you stand there, helpless, and watch it rage. Its power is completely beyond your control. All mankind cannot stop it, but you share in it, and you love it and fear it at the same time.

21

57 So with God. His majesty overwhelms us. He could wipe us out completely. To use a human picture, he could wave his hand and destroy the universe—utterly, not an atom left, all suns gone, not even space remaining. Should we not fear him? Think of the terror we should feel if we did not also know that he loved us. Other feelings begin to mingle with this fear. We respect him. We admire him. We're proud to be able to know even a little about him. When we realize that this God of power actually loves us and planned for us to enjoy this universe, love is added to our fear. The fear of the Lord, for a Christian, is only part—an undivorceable part—of the larger love.

We are concerned about what God says, then, partly because we do fear him. He is powerful; he could eliminate us. We are also concerned partly because we love him. He has all the qualities that attract the highest form of love.

We also are concerned about what God says because what he 58* says is best for us. Use a low-octane gas in a high-compression engine and the motor knocks. Use the wrong detergent in a complex dishwasher and the machine clogs up. That's why the manufacturers send along a manual to tell you how to get the most use and best performance out of your purchase. God created us. He knows what kind of gas we need and what kind of detergent. If we want to run smoothly and perform well, we had better know what the Creator had in mind. It's that simple.

(But there are plenty of people who insist on using "cheaper" substitutes and never seem to realize why the machine breaks down, why life isn't fun. They may run all right until they hit a steep hill or a real dirty dish . . .)

So, even if we want to be selfish about it—and most of us start that way—knowing what God wants of us *is* the way to wisdom and to an abundant life.

God Is Sovereign

Not many people will argue that God didn't create the universe 59 in some way or other, but a lot of people seem to feel that having created it, God has now gone off and left it alone. It

22

follows its pre-set laws, and there it is, and here we are, and so who needs God?

One can look at the universe and come to this conclusion. Some people do. After all, the universe does follow natural laws. Water always freezes at 32° (or almost always, and if it doesn't there's some other law to explain why it didn't and when it will). All science assumes that the universe is predictable. This predictability is impressive. The trouble is that the tools of science 60 fix its conclusions. For example, you can only see whatever is seeable, or if a man only uses a quart measure to measure things with, he's only going to be able to measure things in quarts. This is so obvious that most people can't understand it. Because water has always frozen at 32° doesn't mean that God has gone away. It just means that we have found a way of knowing when water will freeze.

Every so often someone will ask you to prove to him that there is a god. Some of the word's best minds have spent years 61 searching for proofs. Most of their proofs are fascinating, and some are helpful, but by the nature of our human limitations the fact of God cannot be proven. It cannot be disproven either. One of the troubles with people who want proofs is that they want either logical proofs (which their brains can grasp) or physical proofs (which their senses can measure). Since God's existence is of different nature, these tools (brains and senses) cannot grasp or measure him. Our certainty, therefore, is not our brains and senses, but Christ, who shows us the true power 62* and authority of God.

The whole Christian church is based on the idea that God rules. You see this in many of the most familiar statements of the church, such as the Ten Commandments, which begins with the awesome assertion, "I am the Lord thy God; thou shalt have no other gods." Luther explains it "We should fear, love, and 63* trust in God above all things." Also the Lord's Prayer begins, "Our Father who art in heaven," and the Apostles' Creed starts, "I believe in God the Father Almighty, Maker of heaven and earth." This First Article of the Creed is explained by Luther

23

with a number of phrases like "still preserves to me" and "daily provides me" and other words which say that God not only *was*, 64° but *is* and *does*. We sing in the *Gloria Patri*, "as it was in the beginning, is now, and ever shall be," and the *Collects* end with, "who livest and reignest . . . world without end." God rules. 65° He is the Lord, our God; there is no other god. Nothing else comes even close. If we try to put something ahead of God, we are insane and to be pitied, or we are stubbornly self-centered, and basically dead.

What does God want? He wants us to live as though he were our God—which he is.

God rules the whole universe and anything else that may exist. Everything there is, is subject to him. Everything is subject to him not because he tries to keep order, but because he made 66° it *and continually makes it*. God's creation of the universe is not merely a magnificent past deed; it is a continually present act. Like a generator making electricity, as long as it is generating there is current and motors turn, wheels run, pistons slide, machines operate, but the moment the generator stops, every gear, every wheel, every piston, every machine dies. God is the generator, the source of life, the creator of time (each second). If he ever divorced himself from our universe, withdrew the source of life, did not supply the next second of time, then at that moment everything that is would cease to be.

God would not need to come back in anger some day and wipe out our existence; all he would need to do is choose not to create the next moment. Look at your watch for a few seconds. The next second depends on God's willingness to support life, sustain our solar system, continue our universe. The next second depends on him—and the next, and the next. Those seconds ticking by—each one would have been the last one for the universe if God had chosen to stop giving it existence.

The Law

God is God. He rules. The universe obeys him faithfully. The stars run their courses without wavering. Electrons circle their
24

nuclei precisely. Everything science sees follows careful patterns according to simple and complex rules—just as God plans it should. Most of the universe obeys his laws. Perhaps it has no choice. As far as we know, stars and atoms have no will of their own, no freedom within which to operate.

God, however, makes some creatures with wills of their own and allows them freedom of choice. Man is, as far as we are are concerned, the most important of these. Some people say 67 that man is the only creature with his own will. It will be a hard point to prove, especially in a universe that may contain millions of other places where there also is life.

In any case, God has rules for us. Every one of them is 68° designed to help us be what we ought to be, to make our freedom as complete as possible, to give us the highest fulfillment of which our nature is capable, to make our life satisfying. Sounds splendid, doesn't it? The trouble is that nobody ever seems quite capable of believing this. When you remember how tremendous God must be, it seems that only a person completely out of his mind could want to disobey God's rules. To go against God—God, whose wisdom designed this universe! God, whose power keeps it alive! God, whose love makes it enjoyable! Go against God? This is insanity!

Each of us is often insane.

The Milky Way (of which we are a part) hurtles through 69° space at incredible speed, but nobody cares. The earth spins, and we pay scant attention. Our house shakes—we get excited.

A penny in front of your eyes can blot out the sun. People are more ready to look into mirrors than out of windows. Put it any way you want to. The little child is more impressed with the pile of blocks he has built than he is with his father's business.

We humans are like this with God. Those things closest to our hearts hide everything else. We are impressed with our knowledge ("Look, 312 and 312 is 624, and I didn't use paper and pencil"), and with what we can do ("See, I made a rocket"), and with what we are ("Ah, I've been elected class president"), and with our freedom ("If I don't want to dry the dishes, I won't; so there"); so impressed—and so ignorant of God's abilities that we call our weakness strength, our pettiness nobility, our blindness vision, our opinions truth.

We are proud. How we got this way nobody really knows. That we are this way most anybody can see. That we ought to be humble is life's hardest lesson. To acknowledge that God is sovereign, and really mean it, has been humanity's biggest personality problem for all history. We are "by nature sinful . . ."

The prophets of the Old Testament had a disconcerting way of realizing that God had demands he wanted met, that he had rules he wanted obeyed. When they felt that God had made it clear to them that he wanted something done or undone, that was it! Absolutely nothing else made any difference. Men like Amos, Isaiah, Jeremiah ended their speeches about God's demands with the blunt statement, ". . . says the Lord." Period. Take it or leave it. Like it or lump it. Obey it or sin. There it is, like a rock jutting out of the sand around it. There it was: "Thus says the Lord." People were offended. Some were downright mad. A few got the point. When God wants something, you don't dicker with him. You don't hire a lawyer to look for ways around the law. You don't excuse yourself on grounds of incompetence. There just are no excuses when God wants something, because he won't ask without providing you the ability to obey. God is not fooled; he knows whether his command can be obeyed or not. So there you are. "Thus says the Lord." You can't walk away saying, "I didn't hear anything," or, "Who, me?"

There is a real problem about God's laws, and that is one of communication. Genesis says there was a time once in the dim, dim past when God and man understood each other, and calls it a "Garden of Eden." The honeymoon ended quickly. The first child of the first people alive was a murderer. This is the author's way of saying, among other things, that the ideal situation which God originally intended sure got messed up in a hurry. Man had a hard time wanting to listen to God and trying to find out what was God's law and what were his own ideas.

70*

71*

26

God's Law

There are some things which we can say and be sure of. 72
God's basic laws do not change. God's Word is always true.
Perhaps the situations on earth will vary enough so that the law
must be interpreted in different ways at different times, but the
basic law remains. "Thou shalt not kill" is a basic idea. But
when, through no fault of God's, there *is* a war, perhaps killing
may be the lesser of two evils. Perhaps not. Exodus 21:12 says,
"Whoever strikes a man so that he dies shall be put to death." 73
Well now, does "You shall not kill" really mean "You shall not
kill *first*"? In Exodus 32:27f Moses gives the command to kill all
those who are not faithful to God. He felt he was doing what
God wanted. Joshua thought he was obeying God when he had
all living things in Jericho destroyed. The Roman Catholics
thought they were obeying God when they tortured and killed
heretics some years ago. The Puritans hunted down "witches"
and burned them while doing God's will, they thought. The
human element enters the picture. How much it enters varies.
The Bible, by the grace of God, is a remarkably accurate record
of God's dealings with the Hebrews and early Christians. It is 74
the inspired Word of God in matters of faith and doctrine. But
it's not perfect in all areas. Humans were involved in its writing.
And humans, because of their limitations, can never understand
God perfectly.

Although frustrating, this has value. If God and his truth
were always crystal clear, we wouldn't have much use for 75
individual consciences, for growth, for freedom, for love. Most
people would avoid the devil if he walked in on them wearing
a red suit, carrying a pitchfork, swishing his tail, and stomping
his cloven hoofs. If a voice thundered out of the heavens saying,
"This is my law," there would be a bit of scurrying around on
the face of this planet as people hurriedly rearranged their lives.
But there would be little love in the process.

The greatest religious leaders have wrestled with this question,
"What does God want?" They have also asked, "How can we get
the people to obey?"

76   These were Moses' problems at Sinai. He answered the first question with a series of commandments. The second one he never solved. Jesus spent his life answering the first one; and

77*   for the second he came up with the only possible answer. It cost him his life.

Moses and Jesus represent the two basic ways in which people have tried to answer the questions about God's sovereignty. In a way these two persons stand for the two points of view which

78   we call *the law* and *the gospel*. Law is what God demands. Gospel is what God gives. We can never completely do all that God demands, but—with his help—we can accept his gift.

The law is valuable from a number of points of view. It

79   seems to be a necessary step in the development of responsibility. You cannot reason with a baby. When he puts his finger near the electric outlet you slap his hand so that the experience will be unpleasant and say, "No." After a while he learns that reaching for an electric outlet brings pain. On the other hand, the baby also learns that if he does certain things, like smile, or say "da da," he will be hugged and given attention. Such things have the word "Yes" associated with them. Thus he learns to do and not do, mostly because of pain and pleasure, out of experience. Eventually some of these things become habit. This is the law. It is a necessary stage of growth. There is no way around it.

Some day the child will grow up and *may* learn to smile because it makes others happier or because out of love it is the natural thing to do. But this is a maturity most people never reach. In varying degrees they still operate under the law: pain when they fail; pleasure when they succeed.

Becoming Good

80   People who love the law assume that following the law will make you good. Imagine you are an all-powerful leader. You have traveled to a new country, and together with several thousand followers are setting up a society of your own. You want it to be a good society. By "good" you may mean a society where people can be happy, can feel satisfaction with whatever they are doing—a society where there is no crime, etc., etc.

Your experience with people leads you to believe that they have a strong tendency to be selfish, to do what they want even if it hurts others. This will mess up your new society. You will need laws. There will be the obvious laws, fairly easy to apply: "Drive on right side of the street. Do not hit people with coconuts." You will put up stop signs and the like.

After the first hundred people drive through the stop signs, you will add more laws: "Do not drive through stop signs. People who hit others with coconuts will be punished; a list of punishments follows." Now you will need a court to decide whether a fire truck has the right to go through the stop sign, and what to do if someone accidentally hits a friend (or enemy) with a coconut. Such decisions will lead to more laws about fire trucks and unpremediated coconut throwing. After a hundred years there will be thousands of laws and penalties, lawyers and judges, jury systems and jails, honor rolls and gas chambers.

Apparently the only way to make people good is to have enough laws to govern every possible situation, and enough rewards and punishments to make sure they are obeyed in every detail. The perfect society will result from a perfect system of laws, with a perfect set of pains and pleasures to make it work.

Obedience to the law will make you righteous ("righteous" means right with God). This is the theory.

It doesn't work. Your relation to God and to your fellow man must be based on something more than law. Otherwise *even though you are obedient, you will not be faithful. Even though you are helpful, you will not be good. Even though you follow all laws, you will not be righteous.* Why? (1) There is no perfect set of laws known to humans. (2) People are by nature law-breakers. For everyone smart enough to make laws, there are those smart enough to get around them, or stubborn enough to break them. (3) No set of rewards or punishments is strong enough to keep a conceited criminal (or a mentally unbalanced one) from doing what he wants anyway. (4) The highest human actions come from inner motives and not from an outer control.

81°

82°
83

84

85°

29

If you want to see the limitations of the law clearly (as well as its advantages) study the history of the Hebrew people from Moses to Jesus. See how ten commandments developed into the most intricate and complex legal system the world has ever known (*Talmud: Mishnah* and *Gemara*). Listen to what Jesus said about the success of the law in making people righteous. Think about today's world and how many groups are still trying to make the world right purely with a legal system, with rewards and punishments. Even with Christian circles there are many who think that "Thou shalt" and "Thou shalt not" are the basis of Christianity, forgetting that Christianity is different from the law.

86* Luther begins his catechism with the Ten Commandments. They are a wise and necessary beginning. He follows them immediately with the Creed. This is a wise and necessary sequence. For the law without the gospel is dead.

Brilliant though the Ten Commandments are, notice what Jesus did with them.

"You have heard that it was said to the men of old, 'You shall not kill . . .' But I say to you that everyone who is angry . . ." (Matthew 5:21, 22).

"You have heard that it was said, 'You shall not commit adultery.' But I say to you that every one who looks at a woman lustfully . . ." (Matthew 5:27, 28).

"You have heard that it was said to the men of old, 'You shall not swear falsely . . .' But I say to you, Do not swear at all . . ." (Matthew 5:33, 34).

In each case Jesus points out that a whole human relationship is involved, that right living is not merely avoidance of certain actions, but rather is having a constructive attitude. For example, Jesus demolishes the idea that simply not-killing is all that matters. He dramatically makes the point that if you are angry, it is just as bad; if you insult your brother, that too is wrong. Why, if you even say, "You fool!" you have broken the commandment not to kill. It is your relationship to your neighbor that matters, the attitude of your heart. You ruin the right

30

relationship just as much when you cut him down with a sharp word as with a sword. Note how Matthew 5:38 and following go beyond denouncing the wrong way of living and show the right attitude.

Luther, taking his cue from Jesus, shows how each commandment is a guide and measure for us. In his explanations to the commandments, he sketches out the larger area of Christian responsibility. Take, for example, the Fifth Commandment: "Thou shalt not kill." Luther's explanation is: "We should so fear and love God as not to do our neighbor any bodily harm or injury, *but rather* assist and comfort him in danger and want." In the first half of his explanation Luther points out the "spirit" of the law. That commandment never really meant that killing was all that was forbidden, as legalists would say. A legalist is one who follows laws to the letter, the precise meaning. If it says "kill," then that's what it means, no more and no less.) This commandment, says Luther, meant that people shouldn't hurt each other, but to a Christian there is a higher level of operation, stemming out of love. Assist and comfort your neighbor when hurt threatens or reaches him. Why? Not because that commandment says so, or even because the law suggests it, but because if you love your neighbor, this is the thing you will naturally do.

Note Luther's explanation of the Eighth Commandment, "Thou shalt not bear false witness against thy neighbor." The commandment says to a legalist: Do not lie about your neighbor, and please define precisely what you mean by "neighbor." The commandment says in spirit: "We should so fear and love God as not deceitfully to belie, betray, slander, nor raise injurious reports against our neighbor." But for the Christian this commandment is a guide to a much finer and larger area of concern. "We should so *fear and love* God as not deceitfully . . . , *but* apologize for him, speak well of him, and put the most charitable construction on all his actions." ("Apologize" means defend, and "charitable" means loving. Words change.)

87

88

89

31

90*   The Christian is not expected to close his eyes to the imperfections of the world. Even the Christian interpretation of this commandment does not mean pretending your neighbor has no faults; but it does mean that you learn to love him, with his faults, and help him overcome them if you can. Make it as easy for him as possible. Hate the sins, but love the sinner!)

The law is a stage in ethical development, high on the scale. Most people have yet to live up to it. For those who have achieved, there is a higher stage: love. Love does not eliminate the law; it goes beyond it. The law is a teacher which leads us to the next grade; the law is a slave-driver which leads us to desire freedom. The law is part of God's plan.

The Gospel

If the only way we could be right with God were to live in complete obedience to the law, every person would fail. No one would be right with God. God would have to punish the sinner. He would withhold his support. True life would leave. The course of days on earth would run out for the sinner. Death would be the end. The sinner would forever be separated 91   from God, the source of life. This is hell. Hell is the term for absolute separation from God. It is the direct result of men's willful disobedience—that is, if you live under the law.

92   When you think of hell as a punishment, two questions are usually asked (1) Why would a God who made humans the way they are, hold these same humans responsible for acting the way they do? (2) How can a God of love permit the practice of "getting even"? The first asks if God is fair. The second asks if God is loving.

There are many ways of attacking the problem, and all wind up with a mystery. A person can say (if he wants to insist on punishment as a way of getting revenge) that God, at the 93*   moment, is not all powerful. He has an opponent, the Devil. Of course the Devil will be defeated someday, and then God will be the only power, but still. . . . Or a person may point out 94   that nobody is in a position to know whether God is fair or

not. Many a child thinks his parents are unfair when they are being perfectly just, all things considered. We can't know all things, so who are we to say that God makes mistakes! It just looks that way. (And by the way, if God is a God of love, then 95
he isn't fair; he's better than fair.)

Still another answer some give is to say that there is no God. Things just are the way they are. It's fate. You don't have to 96
like it. Funny how some people are more willing to give up belief in God than to give up the idea of revenge!

Or you can say that in order to give man the necessary freedom to love, God also had to give man the freedom to sin. Understood this way, punishment and hell are not the result of revenge but are tied into the nature of sin. Augustine said that 97
God judged it better to bring good out of evil than not to permit any evil to exist.

There are other things that can be said as well, but if you believe in working your way into God's favor by doing right things and avoiding wrong ones, the future looks pretty bleak. It looked bleak to the Jews.

Comes Jesus

Suppose you were walking along and happened to see a colony of ants fighting with each other. If as you watched them you noted that they were doing all sorts of stupid things, that their entire way of life could be improved, how would you go 98
about telling them? Shouting would do no good. You might take a stick and try to push them around. But they wouldn't know where the stick came from, or who was moving it, or that he wanted to help them. The ants would soon go about their business as they had always done.

How would you tell them about your ideas, about yourself? Suppose you could become an ant!

Well, when God wanted to have man know him, he became a man.

For hundreds of years before Jesus' birth, prophets had glimmerings of insight that some sort of deliverer would have to 99* come. The Hebrew people were unable to release themselves from the law and its chains. Perhaps the deliverer would be a king like David—a descendant of David's from the same family line, or at least someone with King David's spirit. Perhaps 100° the deliverer would take the form of a foreign king, who would come in from the outside and straighten out Israel's injustices. Perhaps the Hebrew people themselves, as a nation, could become obedient and then serve to deliver the rest of the world.

What kind of savior would be needed? Would he be young and strong, leading armies? Or would he be kind and loving, winning hearts and lives? Would people listen to him? They 101 hadn't listened to the prophets. They might listen if he came with a show of power, in a burst of splendor. They might, if he drove out the enemy nations.

What would he save them from? From their enemies? From the results of disobedience to the law? (The wrath of God.) 102° Might he save them *for* something as well as *from* something? To lead the world? A light to enlighten the gentiles (non-Jews)?

One day in the history of mankind God chose to speak to 103° men in terms they could best understand. His Word took human form, was personified. The Word became flesh (incarnate).

You know the story of Jesus' earthly life, from birth to ascension. He was a baby, just as we were, equally helpless, equally in need of care. He was a child, just as we were. He went to school, had friends, probably had enemies. When he was a young man he learned a trade in his father's carpenter shop.

Then he became a teacher, the wandering kind, as many were in his day. He got hungry, sleepy, tired. He was happy and he was sad. He was delighted and disappointed. He had men friends and women friends, rich ones and poor ones, good ones and bad ones. He grew angry and he loved.

He was ignored, misunderstood, followed, hated, killed. When they crucified him he bled. He hurt. He died.

104° Jesus was human.

Jesus was a real person. There were some things he didn't do that we do. He was not drafted into an army; he did not
34

marry and settle down. He lived in a conquered country, saw more poverty than we'll ever see, lived in a different kind of climate. But Jesus' experiences with people, basically, were about the same as ours. He knew city people and country folk, wealthy and poverty stricken, healthy and sick. He got along with intellectuals and the ignorant. He chatted with prostitutes, traitors, and thieves, as well as with military experts, congressmen, church leaders.

Jesus knew people.

Although Jesus was human and lived with humans, something about him was exceptional. Something was different. He was uniquely related to God. All through his life he was acutely conscious of this. He and God were close. 105*

Some people feel closer to God than others. Some times you feel closer than at others. But Jesus was closer to God than any other human being has ever been. He was so close that he could say, "I and the Father are *one.*"

This means more than that they are in complete agreement. They are one. This is most certainly true. This is most certainly confusing, too. How could Jesus be God and still be a 106 man? How could he pray to the Father and still be God? How could he really die if he was the source of life? Was he ever really tempted to sin as we are, if he was divine? Did he know in advance all that was going to happen to him, including the resurrection? If so, except for the physical pain, why did he worry about the cross? If Jesus was God, then where was God while Jesus was on earth? How could Jesus commit his spirit to God as he died, if he was God? And on, and on, and on.

Some folks believe that Jesus didn't know what he was talking 107 about. Mental hospitals have lots of patients who think they are God. But get to know Jesus and you won't think he was insane. He gives the assurance that he was the sanest person who ever lived. (Maybe the only one.) His words, his life— all that he was echoes what he said. If ever a person knew what he was talking about, Jesus did. People who get to know him have so much confidence in his authority that they would trust him though all the universe seemed to be opposed.

35

That Jesus was both human and divine is clear in our experience of him. Beyond this, we are faced with a mystery, but not a contradiction. The mystery begins with the moment of conception. The mystery continues through the ascension. From the time he was conceived until he returned to God's fullness, he was both the son of man and the Son of God. This we know on his authority and our experience.

Jesus was divine and human in one personality. You can't split him up and say that when he prayed, he was human; when he healed, he was divine; when he died, he was human; when he rose, he was divine. We know that he was one person, and that he lived a real, historical, human life, but uniquely related to God. He was divine.

108°   When we call Jesus the "Son of Man" or the "Son of God" we are using special terms with meanings different from ordinary use. As he used "Son of Man" it was a term into which people could read as much or as little as they chose. It was a term that would make his listeners wonder, "Who is he? By what authority does he speak?"

It must have been a fascinating mystery to walk around with Jesus as Peter and the others did, wondering who he was. Obviously human, yet obviously more than that. Was this leader of theirs a great teacher? Surely. Was he a great prophet, like Elijah or Jeremiah? Was he possibly a man sent by God to prepare the way for the Savior (Latin word), the Messiah (Hebrew word), the Christ (Greek word)? Or maybe—no, it couldn't be, could it—that this Jesus himself is . . .?

One day Jesus asked Peter, "Who do people say I am?" Peter told him some of the answers: teacher, prophet, even Elijah (the traditional man to prepare for the savior).

"Peter, who do you think I am?" Did Peter dare to say what he was beginning secretly to believe? He did. "You are the Christ, the Son of the living God."

Jesus answered that God had shown this to Peter; and on this he would build his church, "and the powers of death shall not prevail against it."

36

This statement gives us a new basis for our relation with God. We are accepted as members of his church in a new covenant. Let us look at the idea of a "covenant."

The Old Covenant

The Bible tells us that a man named Abraham was one of 109*
those who early tried to lead others to God. He knew that God loved him; and Abraham loved God. God was delighted. He promised Abraham that if Abraham would be faithful in his love for God, then Abraham would be a satisfied man.

This faithful relationship between God and Abraham was called a *covenant*, a promise to be faithful. Another word for covenant is *testament*. In the history of the Hebrews and of Christians there have been two such faithful relationships set up between humans and God. The first comes into focus with Abraham. The second with Jesus. They are both based on the promise of faithful love. They make up the most important events that ever happened to the human race. The story of the first covenant and what happened to it is recorded in the Old Testament. The story of the second covenant is recorded in the New Testament, and it is still going on in you.

It is the story of a complete change in the way that we are related to God, a change God himself made.

The New Covenant

The old covenant says that people can come into a right relationship with God by completely obeying the law. When God sees that they are obedient, then he is willing to accept them.

The new covenant says that people come into a right relation- 110*
ship with God quite apart from success in keeping the law. God gives them this relationship when they trust in him.

Does it seem like a small difference, the difference between these two covenants? The difference boiled down to two words at one time in history—even one word. The Roman Catholic Church said that man is justified by his faith *and works*. Luther 111*
said that man is justified by faith *alone*. Is this quibbling? The words are not important in themselves, but they stand for com-

37

pletely different points of view. The one is Old Testament legalism, which leads to utter frustration and complete death; the other is New Testament love, which leads to joy, satisfaction, and true life.

The new covenant says that man cannot save himself; he hasn't got the power. Jesus showed that he knew the facts of life. Much as we humans might wish it weren't true, much as 112* we wish we could do anything we set our minds to, the facts of history and humanity make it clear to all but the conceited, ignorant, or insane, that man cannot rise above his human nature. He cannot reach the perfection of God.

113 This is one reason why Christianity is superior to all other religions; it fits the facts of our life. It starts off right where we are, not pretending something untrue, not dreaming about some hazy future or unlikely past. It is realistic.

This is facing up to the facts in a way the law never did.

If man cannot save himself, become right with God by him- 114 self, then obviously God has to do it for him. Jesus said that God does. God cannot relax his standards of what is right. God cannot do wrong. In theory, God could do anything. Because God did it, it would be right. But in God "right" is tied up with "love." It is God's nature to be loving.

115* It is not loving to let people do what they want to and accept their mistakes. It is loving to insist that people should do what will bring out the best in them.

God cannot love us and at the same time relax what he wants of us and for us. What he can do is forgive us when we fall short, help us without taking away our freedom, adopt us as his own even though we are short of the perfection he must insist on.

Jesus said that God does this. It was God who sent Jesus to us while we were still filled with disobedience under the law. It was he who showed in Jesus' life how much he would forgive. It was God who through history and in Jesus helped everyone who wanted help. It is God who has prepared for us a place in his kingdom, as his sons and heirs. All this he has done and is 116* doing without compromise, without lowering his goals, his standards, his love.

What could you give God to earn this from him? What value to him are your possessions—to him who made and runs a universe or more! What value to him are your spotty good deeds—to him who is perfect in every deed! What value to him is your struggling intellect—to him who is Wisdom! Even your faith cannot be given him as a payment, because it comes from him to start with. What can you pay a person who has given you everything? Nothing! So stop trying. 117°

God doesn't want payments. Love doesn't ask payments. If you love a girl, you don't do so because you get thirty-one kisses in return, and wouldn't love her for only twenty-seven. If you love someone you don't love them *because* they love you. You love them—and hope they'll love you, too. God loves us because he loves us because he loves us because he loves us. 118°

(When we say we love God *"because* he first loved us," this doesn't mean that we try to balance love out, but it means that if we didn't know his love we wouldn't know what love is.) 119

It is very difficult for God to convince people that they should stop trying to earn their way into his favor. This is the way people normally do things with each other. Since people develop the ideas of right and wrong, good and bad, through the pleasure or pain certain actions bring, they also learn to like and hate as a result of pleasure and pain. If someone *shows* that he likes you, you learn to like him in return. Then you show him that you do, and he learns to like you even more. We judge people by what they do, by their fruits. 120°

Every nurse knows that her male patients will tend to fall in love with her for a while. A man is sick in a hospital; he is worried; he is helpless; he is alone and perhaps near death. His nurse does things for him. She brings food, straightens out the bed, rubs his back to keep up the muscle tone. She puts her cool hand on his hot forehead, checks his pulse, is attentive, tries to cheer him up. This is her job. She does it because she likes people.

She has been nice to him when his whole self needed it. He begins to love her. The emotion goes away after he recovers—not entirely, perhaps, but enough to let him leave the hospital and take up the normal life of a healthy man. In the hospital, the nurse earned his love.

Someone has said that the only love money can buy is that of a puppy. You have a little dog. You feed him, give him shelter, and play with him. He likes you. Even if at times you whip him, ignore him, are a little cruel, he'll still like you. You have earned his love.

Date a girl (assuming you are a boy). Bring her flowers and candy, take her to soda shops and movies, open doors for her and be attentive. Probably she'll like you. You earn her love.

Work well for your boss. Stay after hours for extra work, be cheerful and aggressive, get the job done right. He'll like you. You earn his regard. And so it goes. This is the way human experience seems to be. Even between children and parents, between man and wife, it seems to be this way. The relationship is built of the things you do.

121° Then along comes God, and through Jesus he says, "Not so with me. You cannot earn my love. I do not want to judge you by what you do or don't do. I love you because I love you." No wonder human beings have a hard time understanding the new covenant. It's not the way they are used to thinking.

Remember, though, that this is God and his love. We know he is infinitely greater than we are; so is his love. He can love his way; we scarcely can.

Then there is the question whether love is really love if it can be earned. The Greeks had several terms for love. They 122 had a word for God's love and a word for physical love and a word for brotherly love. We lump these different qualities into one word, "love," and get into trouble with our meanings. When love demands or expects something in return and will not continue without it, is it love or something less?

Then, too, God is in a different working position from human beings. He is the initiator of all things. He starts them. He

40

keeps them going. "He daily provides me abundantly with all the necessaries of life. . . . All which he does out of pure paternal, and divine goodness and mercy, without any merit or worthiness in me" (Luther). Only God can do this. Only God needs nothing to keep him going. Perhaps, then, only God can originate true love. This too must start from him. 123*

If you have to know God's love before you in turn can love your neighbor or yourself, then our patterns of life need some rethinking. People go about frantically trying to earn each other's love. Nations give economic aid, technical assistance, etc., etc., trying to win each other's favor. If they have not yet recognized God's love, no wonder they do not succeed.

No wonder so many marriages break down; the initial romance doesn't carry through. No wonder people hate and steal and murder and are cruel, or just indifferent and cold. No wonder world brotherhood doesn't come about by way of communism or democracy or socialism or through any other *ism.* No wonder society continues injustices. There can be no love until people accept God's love. It starts with him. *It has to start with him!* 124*

Even in the churches some people are trying to earn his love, attending all services, doing whatever they find to do—baking, cooking, sweeping, meeting, speaking not because they love God but are trying to earn their way to God's favor by being active. Such people have not yet realized what God's love is like. They don't yet know the new covenant. This is tragedy. Here at hand is the gospel of Jesus Christ, that God so loved the world that he *gave* . . . and all over the world, even in churches, people are still trying to work their way into his favor. Sometimes it seems that the whole world is off base. We seem determined not to understand. This is sin. And all the time, God is loving. 125*

Read Luther's explanation of the Creed. Man does nothing. God gives everything.

How about my faith? Does God give me that? Yes, he even makes faith possible. We didn't say that he gives you your faith; he makes it possible. You could have no faith if God 126*

41

were not faithful. You couldn't believe in him if he weren't believable. You couldn't follow him if he didn't lead. Faith is not something you build like a city or a bridge. Faith, in the Christian sense, is a relationship. Your faith is a you-God relationship. Since you can't find him, but he comes to you, you can hardly take credit for it. In that sense, even faith is from God.

Well, then, what about the people who don't have faith in God. Is he to blame? Of course not. He is to blame only in that he gave them freedom to reject him. This is not a defect; this is a virtue. If they choose to reject him, that's their fault.

Of course there are many angles to all this that we humans do not understand. What about the people who never heard about God's love in Jesus? What about the people who have a glandular deficiency or brain tumor or some physical reason for being warped in personality? What about . . . ?

We don't know. One is reminded of Job, who asked similar questions. The answer God gave him, you remember, was in effect: When you, Job, can arrange a universe, make and break kingdoms, organize the solar system, etc., etc., etc., then ask questions. The point is not that you shouldn't ask questions, but that, as a human being, you can't know answers to them.

All these questions and answers (or lack of them), all this talk about love and faith is really not important once we know God's love and personality. When you are comfortably sitting on a chair you don't raise endless questions about whether it is there or not, or how it is constructed. If your purpose is to sit, and your need is to sit, and your joy is to sit, it is enough to be sitting. If you know God's love and are secure in it, then questions about faith and love and most everything else are fun, perhaps, but not important. The important thing is that God and you are in love.

The Atonement

You know the facts of Jesus' death and resurrection. How he suffered under Pontius Pilate, was crucified, dead, and buried.

42

You know how on the third day (counting both first and last) he rose again to life. What was the point of all this?

Christians have known from the moment of the cross on, that there was more involved than the fact that a good man was killed. It was the "Son of God" who was killed, and because he rose to life again, a lot, lot more is involved. The whole process is known as the *atonement*.

What did God do? What did he accomplish in Jesus' death and resurrection? There are a number of things involved. Some church people emphasize one more than others. Here are a few:

1. God showed how far he would go in allowing man his freedom. Even though we killed his revelation of himself, his Son, he did not interfere. 131

2. God showed us an example of what people do in the face of Truth and what Goodness should do in the face of natural man. God made it clear that people, by nature, will try to get rid of that which is good. He also showed that Christians, like Christ, may need to go to their deaths—with forgiveness—as examples of the way right operates. 132*

3. God paid the price of the law so that we could have the gospel. The old covenant was still in force. Under it people owed God a great deal, more than they could pay off. He had to punish them. You cannot wipe out a legal contract just because you feel like it. God did not ignore the contract. He sent his Son, who was a perfect man, following the law perfectly, doing even more than the law required. Jesus was so perfect that when he gave his life, he paid the price in full for all man's debt to God under the law. The old covenant was paid off. Jesus had brought the new covenant. His death made it possible. He *redeemed* man from death and the devil. He saved us. 133*

4. God showed man that there was life after death. There was no way for man to be sure of this until Jesus proved it by dying and rising again. 134*

5. Jesus fulfilled the highest form of worship then known to man. According to Jewish worship, no one can enter the presence of God except one person on one day after certain prepara- 135*

43

tions. On the Day of Atonement (Yom Kippur) the high priest, who was the most perfect human the Jews could find, went through elaborate cleansing ceremonies. He then sacrificed the most perfect lamb that could be found—without spot or blemish (a symbol for perfection)—and entered the holy of holies of the Temple (the symbol of God's presence), and asked God's forgiveness of the Jews for another year.

136°   Jesus, the perfect high priest for us, offered the perfect sacrifice, his spotless self (as the "Lamb of God"), entered into the presence of God (remember when he died that the veil of the Temple hiding the holy of holies was split), and then in the presence of God asked for man's forgiveness, for all time. (This act was for all time. We do not need to arrange to have it repeated, nor could we.)

137°   6. Exactly what happened in Jesus' death and resurrection is a mystery, but we do know that in Jesus' experience of death and resurrection something vital happened in which we share. We, as believers in Christ, share his experience. We who are baptized *into* him (note that word) therefore are baptized into his death and resurrection, too. Now that we are branches of his vine, we no longer die like lost humans, but die like Christ; and since we are his and in him and he in us, we also shall rise again to new life as Christ rose again to life. In the Order for Public Confession we say, "Whoever eateth this Bread and drinketh this Cup, firmly believing the words of Christ, liveth *in* Christ and Christ *in* him, and hath eternal life." This union with Christ eludes human definition (Romans 6:5-11).

138°   To atone for something means to make up for it. It is clear that in Jesus' death and resurrection he made up for man what man could not make up for himself. Through the purpose and power of God, Jesus saved us from death and for life with God. In this we see the tremendous love of God, in that while we were yet sinners, he sent his Son to die for us. God so loved the world.

It is human to ask which idea about the atonement is right. But that isn't the right question. They do not contradict each

44

other. Each gives a true but incomplete picture; no one alone is a sufficient explanation. All of them put together are probably not a sufficient explanation. God is always doing more than we understand.

The church uses two terms to distinguish between what God does for us and what we do in relation to God. Something God does for us is *sacramental;* something we do in response to God, especially in worship, is *sacrificial.* Believing that there is more 139 to God's action than to our response, the Lutheran services are mostly sacramental. Two of God's actions through the church are so important that they have been set apart as the two sacraments of the church. As you know, they are baptism and Holy 140 Communion. (The Roman Catholic Church has seven sacraments; most Protestants have two.)

More will be said about the sacraments in this book, but here it should be pointed out that both sacraments emphasize the work of Jesus in his atonement. Baptism is related to the forgive- 141 ness of sins, freedom from death, and embodies salvation (being saved) for those who believe and are baptized. Holy Communion does the same.

We share in the experience of Jesus' death and resurrection (see # 137). By baptism we are united with Jesus in this special relationship. In Holy Communion we share this fellowship with other Christians, and renew our relationship with Christ. As Luther says, the words of the Sacrament assure us that "the remission (forgiveness) of sins, life and salvation are granted unto us in the Sacrament. For where there is remission of sins, there are also life and salvation."

The church constantly emphasizes Christ's work and teaching. He is its center. It is made up of people who take him seriously. Of course, church members are just as human as anybody else; they make lots of mistakes, are proud, stubborn, narrow-minded, 142* and have the defects others have. But if they are really church members (in Christ's Church, not just on some congregation's roll), they have made Jesus their Lord. In their faith they are united in him—in a position to accept God's gracious love.

45

Jesus is the center of the church because he started the church for those who saw God in him. Our final allegiance is to God, the total God who is not only Jesus, but also the Creator and Guiding Spirit of the universe.

143   We are Trinitarians. (*Tri* means three.) We recognize in God three persons (Trinity). All three have always been and always will be. So, thinking of what the different persons of God do, the Nicene Creed can say that the Holy Spirit comes from the Father and the Son. And the Apostles' Creed can say that Jesus Christ was conceived by the Holy Spirit—and there is no contradiction. Does it all sound complicated? Sure it does. The important things to remember are two: (1) God is a real person in whom you can believe and whom you can trust. (2) Problems that arise when we think hard about the nature of God have been wrestled with by great human minds for many generations. Many problems will never have clear answers, because we are human.

144   These little points of logic are interesting to think about, *but the point of your religion is to have you meet God in person.* Whenever you do, the experience will wipe out all concern for little answers to clever questions.

The Resurrection

If God did not give Jesus life again after death, if Christ has not been raised, then our preaching is useless and your faith is useless, and in fact we are saying false things about God (1 Corinthians 15:12-22). The whole Christian church is alive because Christians are sure that after Jesus' death God gave him life again.

It had to be this way. But even if it didn't have to be, it was. All people who are not Christians explain away Jesus' resurrection (means "rise again"). If they believed the story as it stands, they would have to be Christians. If you accept the resurrection

145*   as a fact, then everything else Jesus said, did, and was must be true. Some people don't want to believe this, so the fact they try to get rid of first is the resurrection.

Some have said that Jesus never really died, that the resurrection was merely a reappearance after he hid for a while. Of course this isn't what the Bible says; it isn't what the church has been saying; and it wipes out the atonement. It just isn't true. 146°

Some people say that the disciples only thought they saw Jesus after his death. They were hoping so much that he would return that their minds played tricks on them. When you get to know the kind of solid men the disciples were, this, too, makes no sense. They weren't unstable characters; they were very down to earth. Besides, this wasn't seen by one or two men; hundreds saw Jesus alive again. Some people say that Jesus was alive again all right, but as a spirit, who only appeared to have a body, like a ghost—in the way we use the word today. Again, the Bible stories deny this. He ate, he walked around, he had a very real body. There were some things different about him, but his body was very real. 147° 148

Some Christians, on the other hand, have leaned heavily on "proofs" that Christ rose again. There are some good ones. The whole Christian church is built on the fact of the resurrection. You don't build a church like this one, which has lasted two thousand years so far, and inspired millions of people to give their lives for their faith—you just don't build something like this on a fake story. Then again, all the people of the early church who went around preaching and teaching this good news of the resurrection all did so while eye-witnesses were still living. If there had been anything false about their stories it would have been found out, because every new hearer of the event questioned it, it was so unusual and amazing. The fact of the resurrection is so different from what humans would have expected to happen that even the disciples doubted at first (all of them, not only Thomas). Another "proof" is that these early Christians, who were mostly Jews, and who therefore held the sabbath (Saturday) as the most holy day, suddenly dropped their celebration of the sabbath and began to worship on Sundays. Something tremendous must have happened on a Sunday to make such a change possible. It was the resurrection of Jesus. 149° 150 151

All these ideas are interesting. But nobody believes the resurrection because of proofs, or disbelieves it because of lack of proof. As far as facts of history go, it has plenty of proof. But this is beside the point. You will believe the resurrection because 152° the authority of God in the Bible, in Jesus, in the church's witness, and the power of the Holy Spirit working in you tell you this is true. If you trust God's Word, if you trust Jesus, if you trust the chief ideas of your church, if you trust the Spirit of God which makes you want to believe, then you believe. To put in another way, when Jesus is real to you, and you in your experience know he is alive, that's what matters, isn't it? This is the resurrection, in your life!

Our preaching becomes useful. Your faith is trustworthy. Your life is hopeful. God is your Lord. For you, who believe in the life after death, all things fall into place. You who are baptized into Jesus and his death have also been baptized into his new life. The life that God gave him is yours, too.

Your questions aren't all answered. From time to time you will have some doubts. Naturally. But they won't upset you very long, and they won't change your life. God did give you a mind of your own and the freedom to use it. So use it. One of 153 the greatest Christians who ever lived once prayed, "God, I believe; please help me get rid of doubts." Often we believe with our whole selves, but doubt with our minds at the same time. It's confusing, but it happens.

154° A doubt really does not show lack of faith. Doubts come from the mind, the intellect. Faith is in the soul, the heart, the whole person. You could even say that a doubt is a sign of faith! Anyhow, all great men of Christianity have had both faith and doubts. Like swimming and football, like law and love, like peaches and apples, so doubt and faith don't operate according to the same rules, don't play on the same field.

After the Resurrection

Since Christians have Christ's life in them, and will also live again, we are interested in knowing what sort of body we shall have after our death. What sort of body did Christ have after he rose again? This should shed some light on our future.

Again we are dealing with something beyond human experience. Again we don't have words to give the descriptions. The church has hit on the term, a "glorified body," to describe Christ's body after the resurrection. This is useful. It points out that although his body was obviously still a body, it was somehow different. If you add up all the experiences of the disciples with Jesus after the resurrection, you get the feeling that Jesus had a body of different qualities than he had before. He was recognizable, yet different.

The discussion of what was different, and how it was different, could go on and on, and we wouldn't get very far. Paul sums it up (1 Corinthians 15:35-58) by saying that there is a difference, and that the earthly processes of decay and getting old and things like that don't apply to the new life and new body. Don't worry about it, he says. Just be supremely happy that you will have a resurrection of your body, whatever qualities it may have.

Some intelligent men asked Jesus one time, "What's it going to be like in heaven? Will there be a continuation of marriages? Suppose you've married more than once; which mate will you have?" Jesus' answer was something like, "Look, your question immediately shows that you aren't even thinking in the right terms." As he told Nicodemus, "If you don't understand what's going on on earth, how can I explain this kind of thing so you will understand?"

The Creed only says, "the resurrection of the body. . . ." When God gives you life again, it will be interesting, won't it, to know the answers. Something to look forward to!

Several weeks after Jesus rose from the dead he rejoined the Father. Since we have traditionally thought of heaven as being up, we say he ascended (went up) to heaven. "Up" is a term to be used in space, but God doesn't move around quite like we do. However, it gets the point across. Jesus ended the particular part of his earthly life that was physically visible. (Artists like to paint pictures and it is very hard to paint a

49

picture of a glorified body rejoining God in heaven. If you like
159   pictures, remember their limitations.)

160   Jesus is God. Some day, when God's judgment of this form of
life is to be final, the Christ who lived with men, as a man knew
our situations and died for us, shall be our judge.

How absolutely wonderful that God doesn't decide about us
from way off somewhere in complete uncompromising goodness;
that he doesn't sit somewhere high up, like a judge on a stand,
viewing us objectively, without hatred and without love. God
has come down and lived our lives and knows what we face and
how we face it. When he created us, he knew what we were like.
But after we sinned—in our freedom—he had to learn what *that*
161   could be like. It cost him dearly to learn. But he found out, and
now knowing, he can judge us in love.

(The paragraph above is full of human terms, and it misses
the truth by at least as much as the English language is different
from God's words, and a human writer is different from God's
revelation. But the point of it is true. "He shall come to judge
the quick [living] and the dead," "in order that I might be his,
live under him in his kingdom, and serve him in everlasting
righteousness, innocence, and blessedness; even as he is risen
from the dead, and lives and reigns to all eternity. This is most
certainly true.")

The Trinity

We've talked a lot about God's love because it is the focus of
all Christianity and all life. If this isn't understood, nothing is
understandable. This love is most clearly seen in Jesus. God
didn't start loving when Jesus was born. He always loved. Jesus,
the Christ, is the expression of God. He and God are one. Even
before earthly time began, God was the Christ; he was by nature
162°   saving. *It is in the timeless personality of God that if anything
separates from him, he tries to save it.* This is God as "Christ."
And so we can say that the Christ has always been the expression
of God, and always will be. Jesus could rightly say, "Before
Abraham was, I am." We can rightly sing, "Glory be to the
50

Father, and to the Son, and to the Holy Ghost; as it was in the beginning, is now, and ever shall be, world without end. Amen."

It is also our experience that God lives in us, that we are united with him in a way which we cannot explain. It is our experience that God is working to improve us. He calls us into a fellowship of people who have the same experience (the church). He is the head of this fellowship. He is active within it in a special way, and he is also active outside of it. *It is in the timeless personality of God that he is busy doing whatever* 163* *is needed to achieve his desires.* This part of God's personality, this "person" of God is God as "Holy Spirit."

And of course God is the Creator, the Father of all that is. He is the Father of the universe in one sense, and the Father of his human beings in another sense. *It is in the timeless personality* 164* *of God that he is creative and fatherly.* This is God as "Father."

These three cannot be separated. Unitarians say that we believe in three Gods. This is nonsense. But we find it true to the witness of the Bible, convenient for discussion, and natural in our 165* experience, to recognize the one God in three ways: as the Creator and Author and Father of all things; as the Savior, Redeemer, Son of God; and as the Gatherer and Preserver and Activator, the Holy Spirit. We call these three natures of God, the "persons" of God. (If you can find a better term, good for you. You might try; thousands have. No one has succeeded.) We speak, therefore, of the First Person of the Trinity (the Father), etc.

One of the dangers for Christians is the natural tendency to separate the persons of God. God is all three, equally important, equally real, equally God. We believe, as do the Jews, in one God. Most of our Collects deliberately remind us of this. It's so easy to forget. We center our thinking in Jesus, and forget that it is God in three persons whom we worship.

The reason the Christ is so prominent in our thinking is that this revelation of God is so clear to us. We go back again and again to the historical accounts of the time when the Word became flesh. Jesus made God's love clear.

51

God loved Abraham and the others before Jesus. Some knew it. Hosea understood. The man who wrote chapter 40 and chapter 53 of Isaiah understood. But they did not understand as clearly as Jesus' disciples did, or as we do. How could they? They had not yet clearly seen how far God would go to win people back to him. Jesus alone made that clear. He did it in his life, loving all people, no matter who they were or what they had done. But he did it especially by his death, giving his life (God's life) for all men.

Faith

If *love* is the big word of our religion, *faith* comes close behind it. Like all important words it is hard to define, because there are no other words quite equal to it. We Lutherans say we are justified by faith. God takes us into a good relationship with him if we have faith. All through Jesus' life on earth he told people who came to him for help that "thy faith hath saved thee, thy faith hath made thee whole." Jesus made it clear that faith was the basis for his help. The benefits of the sacraments of the church are based on God's promises of what he will do if we have faith.

What is faith? We've already gathered that it is not something you can pile up and store away.

Faith is allegiance. Wilfred Grenfell said that "faith is reason grown courageous." Faith is the realization that God is true— to the point that you will stake your life on it. Faith is your entire life saying, "The god I know through Christ is God; I will have no other gods." Faith is the attitude of a person whose life is saying, "God, I am yours."

Faith is not simply believing that God exists; it is not simply admitting a series of religious ideas; it is not a wild leap into the unknown for the mere sake of jumping; it is not merely something that takes over when your reason fails, or fills in the spaces between facts. True, you have to believe that God exists; you will have religious ideas and probably agree with some doctrines; you will be at ease with the unknown; and you will believe

52

things beyond your intellectual talents. But these do not make faith. Faith is a relationship. It is your dedication of self to God. It is allegiance. It is trust.

In both covenants God's faithfulness is emphasized. No matter what happened, whether the people worshiped idols, broke commandments, murdered, prostituted themselves—no matter what happened, God was faithful. The Old Testament people thought he was faithful because he had agreed to be! Now we know he 169* is faithful because he loves us. When you consider what we are and what we ought to be, this love of God is a miracle.

Our faith is similar. No matter what, we trust him so much that we remain faithful. Our allegiance should never shake. His kingdom should be our first concern. We cannot serve God and let anything else master us. This is faith.

Of course we fail. All other saints have also failed at times. 170* We do waver. We have other concerns that take over the lead. Many of our desires and our habits at times master us. Our faith has its ups and downs. It shouldn't, but it does. When we come into church membership we "promise to abide in this faith," but we don't abide. The church knows we won't, so two minutes 171 later the pastor asks God to strengthen our faith.

When we prepare to take communion we are asked, "Do you trust entirely in the mercy of God in Jesus Christ?" and we answer, "I do so trust." But we don't trust entirely, and ten sec- 172 onds later we are imploring God's forgiveness.

Faith is allegiance, and trust—trust that God will forgive our lack of faith.

Reaction to God

A friend comes up and says, "I just made a hizzlewhat." Never having heard of a hizzlewhat before you probably couldn't care less if he made ten of them. Unless your curiosity overcomes you, you shrug your shoulders, say something polite, and remain indifferent. But if your friend says, "I just made *you* a hizzlewhat," suddenly you are vitally interested, full of questions, eager to know what it is. If it turns out to be something you'll like, you are full of thanks to your thoughtful friend. If it's real special, you immediately begin to think of ways you can do something nice for him in return.

173 Your parents have provided you with food, a house to live in, clothing, affection, some measure of understanding, a place to air your feelings, and a lot of other things that generally make your life more satisfactory. If your parents are honorable, you honor them. If they show their love for you, you also love them. If they have strong moral standards, most likely you do too. But sometimes days and days go by in which you fail to show your respect, and sometimes days and days go by when you take their love for granted and fail to show them that you love them. Sometimes months go by and you have just assumed that they will provide food and house and clothes, and try to understand, and let you talk, and all those things. They brought you into the world, so they owe you all this. You didn't ask to be born. Of course you prefer being alive to not having been born, and in a way they've done you the supreme favor by bringing you into

174 being. Looking at it that way, maybe you are the one who owes them everything!

Time goes by and you get accustomed to the place and the routines and take them for granted. Then one day something happens. The world is especially cruel, or the world is especially beautiful. There is an accident, or a problem faces you whose answer you must have and cannot find. Whatever it is, something happens and you hurry home. The food you've always had is there again. The house which has usually been warm is still warm. Your folks listen to your trouble or your joy. They share your hurt or happiness. They suggest advice that will help. They stand by you, and as they always have, they love you.

What is your reaction? There isn't a human being that sometime or other hasn't felt the same way. Your love for them be-

175 comes overwhelming. "Your heart goes out." There is no questioning of their motives, no resentment of their rules, no thought of obligations. At this moment you just love them, and there is not a thing you wouldn't do for them.

54

Popular songs constantly tell us what we would do for those we love—parents, sweethearts, husbands and wives, loyal friends: "Climb the highest mountain"; "There is nothing in the world I wouldn't do, for you"; "Take all of me"; "I'll do anything you ask." Think of what a person will do for a member of the opposite sex whom he likes. Think of what a person will do for someone who shows him a little attention and a little affection. Think of what a person will do to have the things around him that make life seem worth while. Think of what a person will do for someone who gives him all that matters: something to live for, to die for, companionship, loyalty, love. For these things we joyfully give all. All — joyfully!

When a person recognizes what God is doing for him he joy- fully gives everything he is to God. In those moments of our lives when we are brought up short, and remember that all these years he has set the table, provided the house, listened when we wanted to talk, presented the only true advice, and no matter what we did loved us — in those moments there is nothing in the world we wouldn't do for God. Parents give us the necessary things for living during our childhood years, and then we are on our own. God gives us our parents and the world of necessary things for ever. A sweetheart gives us inspiration and fellowship, love and sympathy, in varying degrees for a number of years. When sweethearts fail, friends fail, parents fail, society fails, and we fail, God remains loyal for ever.

How do you react to a God like that? There was a son, one time, who took everything his father could give him and left home for adventure. He had money and he made friends, male and female. He had good times and he had adventure. You remember what happened. The money ran out. So did his friends. He was alone. The adventure turned sour. Then, as Jesus says, he came to himself (a good phrase), and started home. All the time his father waited and watched and loved. His father knew the world. He knew what was happening. He hurt for his son. (Maybe you have to be a parent before you can understand that.) He would have done anything he could do to protect his son from the hurt, but interfering now, or forbidding earlier, wouldn't have helped. So he waited and watched and loved.

And one day when the son was still a long way off, his father saw him. (How many days had the father stood there on the front steps watching the empty path as it lost itself in the distance? How many hours had tears blurred his vision? When he recognized that figure in the distance as his son returning home, the father ran down the path, and grabbed the boy in his arms.

How do you react to a God like that?

"Father, I did wrong. I'm not fit to be your son. I'll settle for a job around home where I can be near you, and I don't even deserve that. Let me be a servant." And the father? "Make a feast. Prepare a big celebration. My *son* is home again."

What can you say to a God like that? How does your loyalty look, compared with that kind of loyalty? How does your love look alongside of that kind of love? All you can say is, "God, I'm not much, but all that I am, loves you." This is the way the Christian feels when he realizes God.

180° The most important thing to a person in love with God is to be near him. As close as possible. When a couple are in love they hold hands, they talk with each other or communicate in silence. They are acutely conscious of each other's presence. The church uses a word for paying attention to God; it is called

181° *worship.* (The word comes from the same stem as *worth*, so worship is paying attention to something worth while. God sure is.)

182° You can worship God by lying in bed thinking about him fondly. You can worship God by taking him seriously when you make a decision. You can be walking along the street on a fall day, looking at the colors of the leaves and say, with or without words, "Gee, what a beautiful world you made, God!" That's worship, too. Bach wrote his music as an act of worship, because he wrote it for God. A juggler did his routine one time as an act of worship, because he wanted to show God his best talent. Here and there have been men and women who have made homes, collected garbage, preached sermons, and run for political office — all as acts of worship, because they had given their whole

56

lives, you see, to God. Reading this paragraph could be an act of worship. It may not be if you are just thinking about the words or their meanings. But if you are doing it because you want to know more about God, to whom you feel close, then you are worshiping as you read and think and feel close.

Worship

You can worship God out in the woods by yourself. There are times when this is a very wonderful way to do it. There are times when you must be alone with God. There are other times when 183
any Christian will *want to share* his feelings about God. The
most likely place to find other people who feel the way you do 184°
about God is in church. Formal worship makes this sharing easier. It has patterns which are recognized; some of them just grow up, others are planned. The most effective way to worship together is in a situation where everybody knows these patterns. This happens in church services.

One of the chief forms of worship is prayer. Prayer is talking with God. Paul tells us that we should "pray continually." He 185°
means, of course, that we should be in communication with God all the time. Sometimes this will be prayers we have learned as children; sometimes we will use other prayers we have taken time to memorize; sometimes we will pray prayers we make up as we go along; and sometimes we will say nothing at all, but just feel close to God and think about what we feel and what he may want us to do.

Some of the nicest prayers are those in which we simply tell God how much we enjoy something of his world, how much we 186°
like him. Some prayers are prayers of confession, when we un-
burden ourselves and admit our faults. We recognize his de- 187°
mands and our failings, and we are sorry we fall so far short. In some prayers we ask for things (petitions). We may ask for a 188°
clear dry evening for a hayride (but of course a few dozen farmers may be praying for rain at the same time). We may ask for strength to meet a certain problem, or wisdom to know right from wrong. If we ask God to take care of someone else, this is 189°

57

called *intercession* (passing between), so a prayer for someone else is an intercessory prayer.

190   When prayers take on certain fixed forms, as with poetry and music, they are given special names. One name is *Collect* (accent on first syllable). A Collect is a useful form of prayer to learn, because with it you can make up very nice prayers as you go along. This ability eases some of the fear that you may be called on suddenly to lead a prayer, and that all you'll think of is "Now I lay me down to sleep."

191*   Jesus' disciples asked him one day how they should pray. He gave them a sample prayer, called the "Lord's Prayer." He did not tell them to use it all the time, but he did tell them that this was the kind of prayer they could use. His sample prayer was so good that Christians have been overworking it ever since. You have probably heard it so many times that it's hard to get meaning out of it any more. But it is a wonderful prayer and worth studying and copying — and using, too!

The Lord's Prayer

Even though we have prayed this prayer hundreds of times and said it hundreds more (note!), there are ideas in it that are startling every time we realize what they imply. The first two

192   words are "Our Father." Why not "My father"? Because God's children are a family. Each Christian is constantly related to every other Christian; he does not stand alone. Then, too, this is a prayer for the disciples, for the church, for all Christians.

193*   That word "Father" is a startling word. It is a warm word, full of good feelings, of closeness, of rules, and love, too. For the Christian, God is not off somewhere, so great that we cannot approach him. He, the Creator of universes, adopts us as his sons — not playthings, not pets, not slaves, but sons. Because his "Son" became one of us, we are now one with him, and have become sons of God. So Christians say, "Our Father." Nobody else does. They just can't believe it.

The Lord's Prayer goes on with some other interesting ideas. Using it, we pray for things that seem obvious. "Hallowed (holy,

58

dedicated to what is right and good) be thy name." God's *name* 194*
is his character, his reputation. Of course this is good. "Thy
kingdom come." Who is going to be able to stop it if God wants
it? "Thy will be done. . . ." Does this mean that somebody can
prevent God's will from being done?

As Luther says, "The name of God is indeed holy in itself; the
kingdom of God comes indeed of itself; the good and gracious
will of God is done indeed without our prayer," but we pray in
these petitions that it "may be hallowed also by us," "may come
unto us also," "may be done by us also."

You see, we tiny humans are free (because God wants it that 195
way) to use God's good name for dirty language if we feel like
it. We are free to stop his kingdom from coming into our own
lives. We are free to frustrate his will in those areas where he
gives us this freedom. By his permission we can block him. What
a devilish idea! So we pray that we will never never do such
things, but do just the opposite: show our respect by leading
good lives, work to spread his ideas, and be faithful to him.

The Fourth Petition uses an interesting term, "our daily bread." 196*
Food is available to Christians and non-Christians alike. Bread
(used here as a symbol of the basic stuff for physical life), food,
clothing, money, companionship, whatever we need to live on
this earth, are all around us, usually. For us, who know where
the next meal is coming from, this petition asks that we recognize
who is behind all these things and that he not withdraw his
support. For those who don't know about the next meal, who
don't have a roof, who have run out of affection, this petition is
differently realistic. When your stomach is wrenching from
hunger, or you're shivering from cold, or you're down and out
of friends, you are not in a position to serve God very effectively
in this society.

The next petition is another realistic request. It has disturbed
a lot of people, but there it is, and it means what is says. "Forgive
us our trespasses (first syllable accent), as we forgive those who 197*
trespass (still on the first syllable, please) against us." *Trespass*
does not mean stepping on the grass, but it does mean stepping

59

out of bounds. It means debts, but not just in money. It means unpaid obligations of all sorts. It means anything we have done against God or our brother.

198°   The tricky part of the petition is that "as we forgive . . ." The point is this: If you aren't the kind of person who can forgive others, then you aren't the kind of person who accepts forgiveness. In order to be forgiven, you must be sorry and willing to change (not just scared); and if you can't accept this quality in other people, then you don't have it in you, either. Forgiveness doesn't work like a balance scale. This is in the area of love.

199°   This prayer is full of interesting phrases. Here comes another. "Lead us not into temptation." Who or what leads us into temptation? Do we lead ourselves? Is there a personal devil who tempts — with horns and pitchforks — holding up pretty pictures of things we want to do? Does God tempt us to see how strong we are (or weak)? Luther says that this petition is a reverse way of asking God to steer us away from dangerous ground, and to give us strength "to gain the victory" if we should be tempted.

Luther is most certainly right. But there may be something else indicated by this petition. It would be fascinating to know.

200°   "But deliver us from evil" comes right on the heels of the temptation idea. Here is a petition that goes deep. Obviously it asks that God get us out of the things that are wrong. It asks that God save us from our sinful nature, our pride, our disobedience, and from everything in the world that goes against

201   him. It also asks that all our past errors, all the bad habits we have built up, all the mistakes we made whose conclusions have not yet reached us, and all the inheritance we have been born with which may drag us down—that all these chains and weights be broken from us, and we be saved.

Why do we ask these things? Why pray this kind of prayer? Because God is God. Only he can help in things this important.

202   He rules; his is the kingdom. He has the strength to answer these petitions; his is the power. We can't take any credit for the benefits; his is the glory. For ever and ever (which is at least as long as there is). So let it be; Amen.

It's a wonderful prayer. Roll it around in your mind next time you pray it. Fondle it in your thoughts. Compare it with your experience. Your needs fit into it. All men's needs fit into it. No wonder we use it so often.

God Answers

God, who is always faithful, answers prayers. Prayer is your part of the conversation. Revelation is God's part. You "talk" with each other. A question often raised is, "Does God give me what I ask for?" The Bible is full of statements like: "Ask, and it shall be given you." "Whatever you ask the Father in my name he will give you." Are petitions answered? 203*

Two planes are flying over the Pacific. They are bringing home business men from work in Singapore. One plane crashes and all aboard are killed. The other plane arrives safely at Los Angeles. As her husband steps off the plane in L.A., the wife says, "God answered my prayers and brought you home safely." What happened to the prayers of the wives of the men in the other plane? 204

You pray for a clear evening for your hayride and several dozen farmers pray for rain on the same evening. Even though the rains in Spain stay mainly on the plains (and the sleet in Crete lands neatly in the street), in America they fall all over the place. If the farmers get rain, your hayride will too.

How about the man who has a defect in his character, a defect which keeps him from being the kind of energetic servant of God he would like to be? He prays to God repeatedly to have this irritating thing removed; he can't get rid of it himself. "Please God, so I can do your work better, take this thorn out of my life." And nothing happens. It stays there. Surely God wants this man's character to improve. Why didn't he answer the prayers? 205

Sometimes God answers a prayer request directly; then a person can say with confidence, "My prayer was answered." Sometimes the opposite of what was wanted happens, and seeing that the results turned out better than they would have had he gotten his request, a person can still say, "My prayer was answered. God 206

207

61

found a better way of answering it." But many times we just don't know what God is doing, if anything. The most unselfish prayers sometimes seem to get no farther than our lips. It seems that we might as well be talking to a stone idol.

In such times there is only one comfort, but it is enough. The God who made you, loves you. The God whom Jesus showed us, isn't going to ignore your pleas. He'll do something. He will do whatever is best for you, unless you are blocking him. Even then, he'll do what he can — and that's a lot.

In a time of terrible injustices the prophet Habbakuk also asked what God was doing. He found his answer and wrote it down in a picturesque paragraph. "Get a sign, and write on it in letters so big that a man running by can read it, 'The just man lives by faith.'" You know God; he's loyal. If the world seems the same, if your prayer has caused no noticeable changes, live in faith. God is answering your prayer better than you know.

When Jesus promised that God would answer prayer he had at least two things in the back of his mind as he made the promise. One is that the prayer will be made by a Christian, who in love will ask for only those things he believes to be good. The other is that God's answer does not need to be immediate or direct, but as God sees the whole of things, may take a form different from the one expected.

Most church prayers end with "in Jesus' name" or something similar. This is not just a signal to the organist to get ready to play the "Amen." These words are added to indicate to God two things: first, we are praying as Christians and want to ask for things a Christian should be concerned about, for reasons a Christian should have. Second, we are coming to God because Jesus made this possible. If it hadn't been for him we wouldn't offer this kind of prayer: This is a prayer of children to their heavenly Father. No one except a Christian prays like this.

Prayer is a way of reacting to God's love. It is a form of worship. It is a most natural thing to do. God doesn't care how poor your sentence structure is. If you are trying to tell him you love him, he doesn't care whether it is natural for you to call him

208°

209

210°

211

212°

213

62

"Lord, Holy Father, Almighty, Everlasting God" (*preface* to service of Holy Communion), or whether you simply say, "O God." Some forms seem to show more respect than others; that's why we use "Thee" and "Thou." Whatever forms you use, don't let them get in the way of your praying. It's you God wants to hear, not your vocabulary. 214

Service to God

When someone does something for you, whether it is making you a hizzlewhat or giving you your life, the natural reaction is to want to do something for this person in return. Have you ever thought of something you could do for a close friend, something he would enjoy very much? You are full of excitement and enthusiasm. You work hard at it. You get it just right. You present it to your friend. Your friend enjoys it very much. His eyes light up. He beams in happiness. You are happy.

If your friend offers you money to pay for what you've done, he's missed the point. You don't want it. If he says, "But I'd feel obligated to you if I took your gift," he's missed the point again. He finally wakes up and takes your gift and says, "Thanks." He owes you nothing. He has made you happy by taking your gift. You have made him happy by giving it. From his point of view the gift is swell, but even more wonderful to him is the fact that you didn't think of trading something for it; it didn't cross your mind to get paid; you never once were concerned whether he would do something for you. You *graciously gave* your gift. 215

Undoubtedly your friend will do something for you. He'll want to, because you like each other; not because you gave him something. (He has already done something nice for you by accepting your present in the right way.) 216

When God *graciously* gives you something, the same truths apply. He's not looking for payments or trades or exchanges. He is not giving you anything so you will be obliged to repay him. He is giving because he knows you will be happy with his gift. 217

Once you know this, your natural reaction is to take the gift and be happy with it. Knowing he loves you, you want to do

63

218   something for him. What you do for God is worship him and serve him. You serve, not out of duty like a servant, but out of love like a son. The things you do for God are thoughts and acts that are what God wants, that are "good." ("Good" and "god" come from the same word.) These are called good works. They

219°   are your natural response to God's love.

A person who loves God will do good works. They earn him nothing. They aren't done to earn anything. "If I speak with the tongues of men and of angels . . . if I have all faith, so as to remove mountains . . . if I give away all I have . . . though I give my body to be burned (as a martyr) . . . but have not love, I gain nothing" (1 Corinthians 13). And if you do these good works out of love, you aren't even thinking of gain, or earning.

Lutherans feel that this truth is very important. You don't earn your way into God's favor (or heaven). God gives you that.

220°   Your good works are like the fruit on a tree; they just grow naturally on a good tree. The fruit doesn't make the tree good. The tree is already good, or it wouldn't have good fruit. God makes you good. Being good, you will bear fruit. This is a result, not a cause. God is willing to consider you to be good if you are loyal to him and because he is gracious, not because you can show him a large pile of good works. As Paul was saying (and he was just echoing Jesus), *there is no such thing as a good work*

221°   *unless God has already saved you.*

There are lots and lots of "Christians" who haven't caught this truth. No wonder *justification by faith* is the cornerstone of Christianity. It is the whole point of the new covenant.

Your good works are the result of knowing his love. Your life as a Christian will be full of them. Even if you were perfect,

222°   this would simply be the natural result of knowing God's love for you, and therefore you wouldn't even think of taking credit.

Now that you know, through Jesus, what God is like, what he has done for you, how much he loves you, your whole life is an answer to him. Life is just the way God planned it from the beginning. Everything is perfect. Swell! But it just isn't always true, is it? The theories are perfect; the facts disagree.

64

Why?

What is wrong with the world is not God; it is us. For all his love, we are still human. We just don't understand his love fully; we don't worship him all the time; we are not going around doing good.

We like our way better. This is a form of insanity, but we like it. "I know what is better for me than God does." Absolute non- 223 sense! But that's how strong our pride is.

We take our bow and arrow, but we don't miss the center of 224 the target by accident or lack of practice. We aim off center. We miss the mark. This is sin. The little sins may be that we miss. The big SIN is that we deliberately aimed wrong.

It's a bit beside the point (good expression) to rush up to God and say, "I confess I didn't get the full nine points (which is what the gold center of an archery target is worth); I only got two fives, a three, and one nice seven. What can I do, dear God, to make up those sixteen points?" God doesn't care so much about those missing sixteen points (sins) as he does about the fact that you purposely aimed wrong (Sin). 225°

God releases you from sin when you "repent." In the English 226° language there are two words *repent*. One means "to creep along the ground"; the other is "to change your way of life." The first is a zoological term; the second is Christian. Repentance is not creeping along the ground and sobbing, "I'm sorry, I'm sorry; look at me, I'm creeping!" Repentance for sin is saying, "God, I'll 227° try to change my way of life." Repentance is amending your constitution, deciding to aim at the center of the target, turning 228° around and walking in a new direction. You can't repent without being sorry for what you've been like, but you can be sorry 229 without repenting. God forgives the repentant. He'll also help you repent.

New in Christ

When we are willing to admit that we are not gods, confess that we have loused up the works, and ask God to take over, then he makes us over into the kind of persons who can *increasingly*

230° do what he wants. Not all at once. Not all in this life. Increasingly. This making us over is called *sanctification* (being made
231° holy). God's Holy Spirit is the "person" responsible for making us over.

After the sermon, in the Sunday church service, we sing the Offertory. The second lines goes, "And renew a right spirit within me." The right spirit comes through God's Spirit. It can transform us into new persons, capable of good works.

The beginning of the Bible talks about the condition of mankind. Adam and Eve lived in a paradise God had created for them. But the first people on earth followed their own desires instead of God's, and the Garden of Eden was gone. Sin had entered the picture. Man had fallen away from God. Only through the saving of Christ can man be brought back into the
232° right relationship with God. So Paul says, "As in Adam all men died (were separated from God) so in Christ shall all men live (be reunited with God.)"

Adam is a symbol for humans who have sinned and lost contact with the source of life. Christ makes us new men, who have been forgiven and have regained contact with the source of life.
233° Christ lives in the Christian. This is a mystery, but he really does. He is not just equal to the nicer part of our character. As Christians, God's saving person has become part of us and we part of him. The kingdom of God is within us. We can do all things (not we ourselves, but because God's real power living in us can use us as its hands and feet, head and heart). We are new creatures, not like the old Adam, but like little Christs — Christians.

234° Yet we are still human, and sin. There is a constant battle. Daily we drown the old Adam and dedicate ourselves again and again to God (a daily baptism). The fight goes on between what is evil and what is good, but the fight has already been won. The evil in us cannot ultimately overcome the Christ in us, if we stay united with Christ. And we shall stay united with Christ unless (and this rarely happens) we deliberately and persistently tell God to get out of our lives. (This is called the "sin against the
235° Holy Spirit." Anybody who worries about it, hasn't committed it.)

Baptism — the whole thing, not just the water — brings us into this victorious relationship with Christ. As "sons of Adam," as human beings, we were born of our parents, but as "sons of God" we have been *born again* when God's Spirit moved into us. The church's Sacrament of Baptism assures us that this has happened because Jesus promised it would. God's Spirit, of course, is also working with people who are not baptized. We don't know how he can, or the extent to which he can. We do know, however, what happens when a child or adult *is* baptized. 236*

This fight, even after baptism, between the good and evil in us goes to the roots of things. It has been natural to picture the force of evil in human terms, just as we often picture God. Until recently people assumed that the head of evil was a sort of being. 237* They called him the Devil. Artists painted pictures of him: human-like, and as ferocious as possible. Others thought he couldn't look too bad or nobody would be attracted to him. They pictured him as a smoothie. The Persians used to think of two 238 gods, constantly fighting each other. In Jesus' day and for many years after, people took it for granted that the world was full of good beings (angels) and bad beings (demons). But of course 239* the good was stronger than the bad. People today, who have learned to stop thinking of God as a big human, have also begun to stop thinking of the Devil in similar terms. We still use the term Satan to designate the mystery of the evil one in our world.

Every Christian knows from his own experience that there is a battle going on, and he is in the middle of it, and it is in the middle of him. The new man in Christ knows that Christ has gained the victory.

The New Man

The Christian is a new person. The rest of the world may envy 240* him, may hate him. He may be honored, or he may have his goods, fame, family, even life taken away. It makes little difference. He has the kingdom of God. Heaven and earth can pass away, but not God. The Christian, in a relationship with God's Son so deep that words cannot express it, is tied in with God.

Even if heaven and earth were to pass away God will be faithful to the faithful Christian.

241° We are living in a time when people are scared. They aren't sure of themselves. They don't know what they are doing on earth, or where they are headed. Nuclear bombs could wipe out
242 everything. So people rush around, trying to forget their confusion by hurrying, by pretending to be what they aren't, by letting their governments take care of them, by surrounding themselves with noise, by any way they can think of. Psychiatrists tell us that people feel insecure. They feel unable to do what they need to do. They are lonely, even in crowds.

243° You, on the other hand, know you are a child of God. You *know* who you are. You are a sinner, whom God loves and has saved. You are different from the society in which you live. God has made the difference for you. It's not that you've put away your teddy bear and grabbed a hold of God. That would still be a child's way of meeting life. You are putting away childish things. You are a new person, heir to God's kingdom, member of his church, his son or daughter whom he loves.

If you confirm your sponsors' faith, you will constantly grow in this relationship. You are never insecure, for his kingdom will come and you are part of it. It has already begun to come within you. You are never unable to do the things you ought to do, for
244° God works in you and you can do all things that need doing. You are part of his church, which even the gates of hell can't stop. You are never lonely, for all other Christians love you.
245° (They may not all know it yet, but they do.) And God himself loves you, for ever and ever.

Hope

"Love" and "faith" have been two important words in our
246° study. A third important word is "hope." Christian hope is not some sort of wishing-well affair. It is not a childish dream unfit for the facts of life. In our funeral service we mention "the sure and certain hope of everlasting life." Hope is sure and certain. This sounds like a contradiction, but isn't. "Time" confuses us. If something hasn't happened yet — from our point of view —

68

we say we hope it will. But since from God's point of view it may be a certainty, we can end up with a "certain hope." 247°

The Christian's life is built on this kind of sure hope. I believe that I am saved — yet of course only God knows. I hope for the resurrection of my body when I die — yet of course only God 248 knows it will happen. But I know that God knows, even if I don't; so I have a confident hope.

The fact that God knows something will happen — and he never is wrong — doesn't mean that it *couldn't* go differently. He didn't determine everything. We are still free to choose many 249 things, make our own moves the way we want to. He didn't decide a long time ago how everything was going to come out, although he made his plans. But God, knowing everything, can see in advance what is going to happen. 250

On the wall of your livingroom is a light switch. You know the electricity is working, the switch is good, the bulb is good. The light in the room is out. It is fairly dark. A friend of yours comes to visit. He can't see well in the dark. You know this. You also know that he is very polite. You now know as sure as anything what is going to happen. He will enter the room, notice how dark it is. Being polite, he will ask if he may turn on the light. You will say, "Sure." He will reach for the switch by the door and flip it. The light will go on.

Did you make the light go on? Did you pre-destine it? Of course not. But you knew in advance that it would go on. You had fore-knowledge. We are free individuals. God does not pre-destine us. But he knows us well enough to have fore-knowledge of what we are going to do. And he knows the universe well enough to know what is going to happen to us.

Some things he has determined. He has determined, for ex- 251° ample, that anyone who believes in Jesus will be saved. He has predestined, for example, that anyone who is saved will be adopted as his "son and heir to his kingdom." He knows who will be saved, but he has not determined it.

His knowledge is too wonderful for us, so we now live in hope. Confident hope! We don't worry about being saved. We don't worry about heaven or hell. We don't even worry about our faith. 252°

God will do the right thing by us. His decisions will be best, not only for him but also for us. But since everything isn't absolutely fixed, we can keep as close to God as we want to. If we put his kingdom first in our lives then we can stop worrying about other things. "Do not be anxious about tomorrow," said Jesus, "what you shall eat or drink, or what clothing you will wear. God knows what you need. He'll provide it." What we need ranges from "daily bread" to "salvation." It does not include color television.

The Christian lives his life wherever he happens to be, without fear, without too much concern about details. He is comfortable in God's love, secure in God's kingdom, sociable in God's church. Having everything he needs, the Christian can use all his energy serving God on earth — and Mars and Venus, anywhere.

Your Future with God

There may be a war between great world powers at any moment. They seem very big to someone standing on earth. They shouldn't scare you.

The prophet Elisha had a helper. Elisha had done some things at which an enemy king grew furious. The king was determined to kill Elisha. One night Elisha and his helper were camped on top of a lonely mountain. As dawn came up Elisha's helper got out of the tent to stretch. All around the foot of the mountain were soldiers and chariots and horsemen. Thousands of the king's men had surrounded the mountain. They had come to kill Elisha and his helper. The boy rushed back into the tent.

"Elisha, what will we do? There are so many of them!"

Elisha took the boy outside and looked at the heavens above. He said a prayer. "God, open his eyes that he may see."

And the boy had a vision. He saw the skies filled with chariots of fire, endless horsemen, rank on rank, file on file. God showed him, in terms the boy could understand, the power of God.

Those few thousand armed humans on the valley floor? They didn't matter. He was on God's side. So are you. God will take care of you. Sure, you may be killed, but God will still take care of you. He did with Jesus.

70

Before you were born, and were still inside your mother, you probably didn't do much thinking. But if you had you probably wouldn't have liked the idea of being born. You had food, warmth, and a snug little world. You were content. Suppose you had known what was happening when you were being born. Frightening! Great changes! You were leaving your world. Would there be a new world? Would it, too, be warm and comfortable? You didn't want to be born.

Now as you look back, what do you think? Are you glad you were born? You couldn't know in advance about this wonderful world. You would have missed it had you stayed where you were.

Some day you are going to die. Everybody does. We have 255° Jesus' promise that death will be like birth; we will move into a new world which God has prepared for them that love him. Knowing that it is far better than this one, and hoping — in sure and certain hope — that we shall share it, there is no fear of death. The sting is gone for you. The grave has no hold on you. Before Jesus' time, Job asked plaintively, "If a man dies, is it pos- 256° sible that he may live again?" Since Jesus' time we say assuredly, "Thanks be to God, who gives us the victory through our Lord Jesus Christ." We shall live again.

Young people aren't much concerned about death, even though it could come for them the next minute. They're too full of life to care about death. The trouble is that people have a way of putting off caring about it until it has sneaked up on them. It 257 has been said that you should start preparing for death the moment you are born. People don't like to talk about death be- cause they are afraid of it. Christians shouldn't be afraid; they no longer have anything to fear. It may be like being born.

The pictures of heaven that we usually have, have been drawn for us by artists and poets who are older than we, prob- ably closer to death. Most of these people have had a fairly hard and busy life. Their idea of heaven is a place where they can rest! The hymn, *Jerusalem the Golden*, says, for example, "Jesus, 258° in mercy bring us to that dear land of rest." And other hymns say: "O Paradise, O Paradise, who doth not crave for rest?"

"Jesus, still lead on, till our rest be won." The beautiful *Collect for Peace* at the end of the Vespers Service, thinking of both now and the heaven to come, asks that "we may pass our time in rest and quietness. . . ."

Young people don't usually want to rest. Passing our time in rest and quietness seems a real bore. Perhaps you, like the poet Robert Browning, will prefer to picture heaven as a place of continued busy-ness, where the thrill of being about and doing things continues. Heaven is not floating on a pink cloud, plucking lazily on a harp. Even the world's most tired Christian would soon get sick of that. The adult pictures of heaven, which often seem dull to the teenager, fit the adult's desires. The idea of rest also comes from our knowledge that the battle against evil will be over, "the conflict o'er, the battle won." So we sometimes confuse peacefulness with inactivity.

259°

Nobody here really knows what heaven is like. Beethoven, unable through deafness to hear his own later symphonies, said as he died, "I shall hear in heaven." For many people heaven is the promise of getting together again with friends and loved ones who have already died. Each person pictures it differently, to suit his wishes. The author of the last book of the Bible uses a marvelous picture, full of symbols. He takes all the bits of history and scattered pictures of delight that have grown up in the Hebrew tradition and weaves them together.

260°

Jerusalem was their capital city; it was the city of David, their greatest king. In it was the Temple. For the Jew, Jerusalem stood for all that was home. So heaven is called the new Jerusalem, the holy city. All tears shall be wiped away. There will be no sun shining on it (the sun is terribly hot in Palestine), for God will be its light. The walls are built of jasper (very precious) and the streets of pure gold (not just fourteen carat) and as transparent as glass (interesting idea). The twelve gates (one for each apostle) are each made out of a single pearl (how's that for pricelessness?). From the throne of God flows the river of life (in a desert country water is the most precious thing there is; it gives life). And God is the center of the city.

72

Sure, you'd get tired of walking on gold streets. That's not the point. The point is that every person uses the finest and most precious things he can think of to tell others what heaven is like. But the greatest joy, without question, will be that of meeting God "face to face"— like the Prodigal Son, coming home to your Father. 261

(And perhaps on some distant planet in some distant galaxy, 262* where family life is different from here on earth, they know God not as a masculine "Father," but have some other image of him entirely, as he has revealed himself to them.)

What can we say God has prepared for you? Something that "passes man's understanding," something you will be alive in, and at home with. Where is heaven? Not up or down or sideways. We think in terms of space, remember? Maybe heaven isn't some-*where* or even some-*time*. But heaven *is,* and it is for you. 263 You and others and the whole creation will reach fulfillment in "a new heaven and a new earth."

Meanwhile, back on this earth, you have a life to live here. As a Christian you have God's assurance that he will help you live it. Not only will you live it, but if you stick with him he will see to it that you get a full life — full of energy ("enter into the joy of thy Lord"), full of things to do ("filled with work for the 264 Lord, knowing that, because of him, it will succeed"). God is with you always, even to the end of the age, renewing and increasing in you the gift of his Spirit, to strengthen your faith, to help you grow in grace, have patience in suffering, and the hope of everlasting life.

So we live in faith, hope, and love. But the greatest of these is love.

II

MAN AND SOCIETY

YOU BELONG TO SOCIETY

You were born into a family. You did not spontaneously come 265 into being. Without any choice of yours, you became part of a social unit consisting of two parents, possibly some brothers and sisters. There are miscellaneous other relatives also involved. It's your family — whether you like it or not.

You were born into a community. It may have been New 266 York, Winnepeg, Leadville, or Rural Route #3. You will grow up in one or more communities. There will be a civic community—the town in which you live, or the families along your highway. There will be a school community, a church community. You are part of these, influenced by their customs, pressured by their standards, molded by their attitudes— whether you like it or not.

You were born into a nation. Automatically you have the 267 privileges and responsibilities that accompany citizenship. Your nation has control over you—whether you like it or not.

You were born on this planet in this state of development. You have inherited the stream of its history, the extent of its cultures, the injustices of its social situations, the uneven distribution of its wealth. You have to live with Chinese and Russians and Mexicans and Caucasians, with Methodists and Roman Catholics and Lutherans and atheists, with communists and socialists and Republicans and Democrats—whether you like it or not.

Governments and other authorities—family, school, community, church, all sorts—are here and will stay here. You have to live with them whether you are a Christian or not.

Society has rules

All forms of society have rules and customs (mores). If we trace customs back to their origin we discover that there were

75

practical reasons for many of them. The food and diet laws of the Jews, for example, largely grew out of the danger of certain foods spoiling quickly in a hot climate. Customs often started out as ways to preserve the society, either from real physical dangers or from imagined spiritual ones. Many are a mixture of the two. In various societies customs differ. What may be important to one group may be meaningless to another, but most people in a group take their customs very seriously, especially if somehow they have been connected with religion.

269° As times change and society no longer faces old problems, many established customs make little sense. But traditions have a way of hanging on long after they are useless. The idea that a man should walk nearest the curb is a hangover from the time when garbage and junk were thrown out of the second-story windows onto the street. The man would be the one liable to be hit, not the woman. Few people throw out their garbage that way any more. Today the custom is useless (except when some idiot speeds down the street after a heavy rain).

When someone sneezes we say "Gesundheit" or "God bless you." Years ago it was believed that a person's soul was connected with his breath. (In the New Testament the words are often the same.) When a person sneezed it was thought that the soul temporarily left the body. To be sure that no evil spirits took this opportunity to sneak inside, a phrase of blessing was spoken to scare the demons away.

When the Zulu sneezes he takes it as a sign that his ancestral spirit is now in him, working to make him healthier. Instead of saying "God bless you," the Zulu tells his ancestral spirit "Grow." When a Moslem yawns he puts his hand to his mouth to keep the Devil from jumping in. And so on. In spite of our greater knowledge, we still follow the customs, usually not knowing why, using the reason that "it's polite."

270 The Dobu tribe teaches its members that complete hatred and distrust of everyone yield the highest form of society. Certain Iranians, believing that God is already helping them, worship the devil instead of God, to keep him friendly, too.

Shaking hands used to be a way of showing the stranger that you had no weapon in your hand to hurt him. Christening a ship was related to baptism. The inch which we use in measurement was the length of the upper part of one king's thumb. Halloween started out as a religious festival. Easter is dated by 271 astronomy and was named after a pagan goddess! People just assume that social customs and traditions have meaning and are right. To break them is considered wrong.

In some parts of Arabia, the sons of Arab chiefs are dressed like girls until they are in their early teens. Evil spirits might weaken them while they are growing unless the demons can be tricked into thinking they are girls and, therefore, not important! Some Polynesian islanders have the custom of putting the men to bed while their wives are expecting a baby. Elaborate precautions are taken to fool the spirits into thinking that the husbands are really the wives. Once the baby is born and the wife is strong again, things go back to normal. One day some Polynesian is going to say to himself, "What am I doing here in my wife's clothes pretending I'm having the baby?" And the custom will come to an end—at least on that island. Meanwhile, these are the right things to do. Society says so.

Not too many years ago, when a major building was being built, a person was buried alive under the building, to satisfy the spirits of the ground on which the building was built. We do not follow this horrible custom; instead we have ground-breaking ceremonies. In Borneo, among the Dayaks, before the first post is put in for a large building, a slave girl is thrown into the hole. The post is then dropped on top of her, crushing her to death. This is part of the religion.

It is easy for us to see how foolish and how brutal the customs 272 in other societies are, how wrong their ideas of what God wants. It is not so easy to see our own foolishness and brutality. Remember the burning of "witches" in New England? Recall one way "Christians" decided who was a witch. She was bound hand and foot and thrown into a river. If she drowned, she was innocent. If she floated, she was guilty and then hanged! Remember that a few years ago the mentally sick were locked up in the attic? Read today's newspaper and discover how much foolishness and cruelty still go on, some of it in the name of religion. There are people who still believe that God made some races inferior to others. During your life you'll hear lots of people say things like, "If God had wanted women to have purple lips, he would have made them that way." Reminding such people that God made humans without clothing, doesn't impress them at all.

273   A pretty girl walks down Main Street wearing a fingertip length skirt. Not only will heads turn but tongues will waggle. Obviously a cheap sort of girl, the wrong kind to associate with, no doubt immoral! Now give the same girl a pair of roller skates, or a baton to carry. What a difference! She's the wholesome athletic type, clean-cut American girl.

A man ambles down the street dressed in baby clothes. He's off his rocker. Call the police; he may be dangerous. But if he does this the day after the national election, or on Halloween, then he's a good sport, full of fun. Everybody enjoys him.

A man picks up a gun and kills another man. Here is a criminal, one of the worst. He must be killed in return (after a trial). But if there is a war and the same man kills ten of the enemy, he is a hero.

Square dancing is right; social dancing is wrong. Smoking is right when you are old, but wrong when you are young. Driving on the left side of the street is wrong, unless you are in England, where it is right. Wearing only a string of beads around your waist is wrong, unless you are along the Amazon where it is the right clothing. Having a party in the parish house is all right, but not in the church building. At eighteen you are too young to vote, but old enough to die for your country in a war. It is all right for a criminal to be the hero of a movie as long as the ending has him reform or shot. You are out of place in your group if your bobby-socks are rolled down, but in the neighboring school you are out of place if they are worn up.

It is feminine for a man to use perfume, but perfumed hair tonic is masculine.

The ideas of right and wrong which society insists on are 274 often man made. For the Christian to assume that these have some connection with Christianity, can lead him far from the truth. There are examples of missionaries who have insisted that natives living near the equator should dress in New England type clothing because "this is Christian." There are churches which, in the name of Christ, have made African natives with several wives and many children actually choose one set of children and one wife. After the native had become Christian he was expected to throw out his other wives and children. Christians, you see, believe in monogamy (one mate). It is easy for us to assume that our particular way of life, with all its social details, is God's way. Once we believe this, we are in a poor position to appreciate other peoples, to be at ease with Christians in other cultures, even to understand Christianity.

Are traditions right and wrong? Are customs moral, immoral, 275 or in themselves neither?

Is there such a thing as right and wrong? Or is everything 276* relative to the time, the place, the occasion, and who is doing it? Is there anything of which it can be said for all times and all places, "This is right and never wrong," or "This is wrong and never right"?

The author of the Book of Ecclesiastes understood the problem. He saw that many things are called right in one place and wrong in another, right at one time and wrong at another. Everything goes in cycles; you wear pajamas at night, good clothes to school, shorts for play, and formals after six.

Tides, skirt lengths, and civilizations rise and fall. What is permanent? What is true? What is right and wrong? How can we know?

WHAT IS MAN?

To know what is right for man, we need to know what man is. Some people say that man is another animal. All that matters 277

79

is the way he survives, the way he feels. Right and wrong are connected with keeping the race going, enjoying life with animal pleasures. Wine, women, and song, said one philosopher, are what make the good life (for men). Pleasure is god. We are animals, superior animals. The apes and we have descended from common ancestors. (As the zoo monkey asked, "Am I my keeper's brother?") But we are still animals, classified as *Homo sapiens*.

(A lot of people are treating you like an animal. Think of the amount of advertising that appeals to your sensual desires, to sex, to lusty physical pleasure. To be grown up is to be able to do what you want to do, like an animal. Power makes right. Pleasure makes right.)

278 Some people say that man is a machine. The scientist, Pavlov, experimented with dogs, giving them food every time a bell rang. After a while their mouths watered when they heard the bell, even if there was no food. Like those dogs, man can be controlled. Stimulate him the same way often enough, and he will respond the same way every time. Under certain controlled conditions the results will always be the same. Repeat a popular tune often enough and people will begin to hum it. Present an advertising slogan often enough and people will think of that product when they buy. Repeat a lie often enough and people will believe it is the truth. Man is a machine.

(A lot of people are treating you as a machine. They say that if you fail, it is because you need better education. The Chinese communists are treating their whole society as though people were machines. Right represents ability to fit into the machine pattern; wrong is deviation from it. Truth is what happens. How much you produce is what matters.)

279 Some people say that man is a hero. He is noble, virtuous, aggressive. He is making progress onward and upward for ever. There is no limit to his eventual ability. Appeal to a man's desire for perfection and he will become more nearly perfect. Some day a glorious society will exist where everything is magnificent, a society which man has carved out for himself, lifting

80

himself up by his shoes. Right and wrong are related to the upward progress of society. Anything is right that adds to this.

(A few people are treating you like a hero. They are called *humanists,* for they think that humans can be anything. They drive you on toward perfection—as they see it. When you stumble or fall, they urge you to try harder and harder.)

You *are* partly animal-like. You *do* have machine qualities. 280*
There *is* something noble and heroic about you. But you are more than these. You are a child of God.

Certainly you have animal instincts, passions, desires, physical urges. They are part of the make-up God gave you. They are neither good nor bad. If you use them only as an animal does, for his own preservation and pleasure, they may be badly used. If you use them as a child of God, good will result.

You have machine qualities. You do produce things and your responses are somewhat predictable. If you use these qualities merely to get more things for yourself, or if you use these machine-like qualities in others to force them into your patterns, evil will result. But if, as a child of God, you use these qualities for the advancement of society and knowledge, then good will result.

You have heroic qualities. But if you believe you can save yourself and society without God's Spirit, chaos will result. As a child of God, though, you can reach far greater heights than even you may dream of, doing all things through his power.

The Christian has no "symbols for success." He doesn't meas- 281*
ure life that way. This does not mean that he is a failure. In fact he is God's highest human success. The Christian doesn't worry about success. But to get to the point where you don't worry about "status" symbols is difficult when you are in a society which considers them to be all-important.

A lot of people all around us still are not aware of who they are. They are unhappy and don't know it. They keep grabbing for signs of success, but are not satisfied for long. The Christian lives among these people, but is not one of them. He knows who he is and what he is doing.

As a child of God the Christian knows that right and wrong are related to what he wants. Truth is his viewpoint. People didn't always connect God with right and wrong. The gods of 282* the Romans and the Greeks, for example, were not thought of in relation to morality. Religion was the worship of powerful beings who might decide to help people, or harm them, depending on how they felt. The kind of life a person lived had no connection with his god. Each city developed its own customs. "Morals" originally meant the customs of a city.

One tremendous contribution of the Hebrews to world society was the idea that God is concerned about morals, about right and wrong, about people's relationship with their neighbors. Most of the Ten Commandments stress relations between people. Christians go a step farther (the final step) and say that you cannot serve God except by being right to your neighbor!

283* For the Christian right and wrong are not relative. What is good and bad is always good and bad. God does not change his standards. His law stands. It isn't different for the country and the city, for summer resorts and winter offices, for school and church, for boys and girls, for youth and adults. God's law does not vary. Social mores vary; customs around us differ; laws of governments change; but not God's law.

The difficulty arises when we try to decide which are God's laws and which are the laws of society. The Christian has the only possible way of being sure: Love.

The Christian, acting from the love of God, knows he is obeying God's laws in being a Christian. What the Christian does in love is right. The Christian recognizes that he is a part of God's family, as are all other people. He is created into a family situation which embraces all mankind. In his heavenly Father's love he wants to do those things that are right.

284 The Christian has to keep two things in mind as he tries to fulfill God's wishes:

1. God has provided certain standards which we interpret through love, and upon which we act. We see these, for example, in the Bible and in Christ.

82

2. God has also created the kind of orderly world where families, communities, governments, and other authorities are necessary. The Christian has obligations to these, too.

The first of these two items is not new to us. We have examined it in part already. Let's look at the second.

AUTHORITY

Luther explains that God's kingdom is seen in two ways. He calls them "the kingdom on the right" and "the kingdom on the left." The kingdom on the right is God operating through the church. Its job is to spread the gospel and help its members live in God's love. Its power is God's Word. We'll talk about the church later on. 285°

The kingdom on the left is God operating through social authority, the power of government. Its job, says Luther, is to provide for justice and order. Its power is the power of the sword, police and military. Governments operate under the law of God, through laws of their own. 286°

Family, community, state, national, and international governments are ways God uses to punish the evil man and protect the good man in society. All earthly forms of authority are part of this kingdom on the left.

Every Christian, then, has two relationships to maintain. Being a Christian he lives by the gospel, heeding the Word of God. The Christian also is a citizen and a member of many communities. The Christian needs authorities to establish law and when they do, he ought to obey them. Service to God must be performed within the framework of society. 287°

God created an orderly world. All forms of authority exist so that there will be order in human relationships. They are a definite part of God's plan for man's life. Their authority is from God.

When Jesus was on trial before Pontius Pilate (or was it the other way around?), Pilate said, "Do you not know that I have the power to release you, and the power to crucify you?" Jesus answered him, "You would have no power over me unless it had been given you from above . . ." (John 19:11). Jesus meant that there would be no governor and no authority for him to wield, had not God planned it that way. He is responsible to God for whatever power he may have.

288   The *Augsburg Confession,* a basic statement about Lutheran beliefs, says, "Our churches teach that lawful civil ordinances (rules) are good works of God and that it is right for Christians to hold civil office, to sit as judges, to decide matters by the imperial and other existing laws, to award just punishments, to engage in just wars, to serve as soldiers . . ." in a word, to meet the obligations of Christian citizenship (Article XVI, 1 and 2).

289   Luther, explaining the Fourth Commandment, says in his catechism, "We should so fear and love God as not to despise nor displease our parents and superiors, but honor, serve, obey, love, and esteem them." Notice that although the commandment only mentions parents, Luther has expanded this to include all superiors. We honor, serve, obey, and esteem them because we "so fear and love God." What happens if the people in authority

290°   don't love God? What happens if societies and governments use their authority in a wrong way? What happens if you have to break a law of the kingdom on the left in order to live in the love of the kingdom on the right?

There are many times when governments are wrong. Pontius Pilate was wrong. The Roman emperor Nero was wrong when he persecuted the Christians. Hitler was wrong when he slaughtered millions of Jews. The United States has been wrong in some of its dealings with the Indians and Negroes. In your school are teachers who have made mistakes in their use of authority. Even your parents have been wrong from time to time, as you and they well know. And whatever authority is yours, you have misused, too.

What should a Christian do if he has to go through a stop sign in order to avoid hitting a child playing? What should the Christian do if his parents ask him to commit a crime? What should the Christian do if he feels a war is not justified, but his country insists that he be a soldier?

84

Simon Peter gave answer to many questions when, in a similar conflict between the two kingdoms, he stated, "We should obey God rather than man." The gospel is always higher than the law. The kingdom on the right has precedence over the kingdom on the left. If you can't obey both, obey God rather than anything else. 291

When God gives authority to people to use over other people, he does so with the understanding that they will use it justly. If they do not, they are misusing that authority. They must either be corrected or removed from power. When we put people in positions of authority, it is also our job to remove them, not God's. When a government is persistently wrong, it is the Christian's right to change the government. Even revolution may be necessary. 292*

If you ever find yourself in that awful situation, remember that you do not stoop to evil in order to fight evil. This just leads to twice as much evil. God's way is to overcome evil with good. You may be able to do this by sitting tight, resisting evil pressures passively. You may have to take up armed power and use it in love. Luther believed that there could be such a thing as a war that is justified. Thus it could be right to use rifles, bayonets, planes, and tanks. Not all wars are justified. Now that we are confronted with the very real danger of destroying all life with nuclear bombs and fall-out, some Christians are asking whether any war can be justified that requires such weapons. 293*

When there is a clear conflict between the two kingdoms, the Christian knows where his primary allegiance belongs. He must render unto Caesar the things that are Caesar's, but unto God the things that are God's.

Usually the conflict between authorities is not so obvious, not so clearly divided. What if your teacher says one thing and your parents say another? Which authority should you obey? Suppose the adults in your community are against new-style haircuts for teen boys, but the gang you go out with insists on them? Which authority should you obey? Suppose you want to stay out until midnight on a special Saturday, but your father 294* says, "Only till eleven"? Which authority should you obey? What is right?

Then there is always the problem of the community customs and traditions. Which is to be done, attend the traditional family Thanksgiving dinner or go to the traditional football game and cheer for your team? Or, you are a Lutheran living in a conservative non-Lutheran neighborhood. Card playing is considered a form of gambling unfit for Christians. You play merely for fun. Should you play cards in that neighborhood?

If various community traditions interfere with either the commandments of God or the gospel of Jesus, clearly they should be avoided. The Augsburg Confession, speaking chiefly about church traditions, says, ". . . men are warned that such observances (traditions) do not justify before God and that no sin is committed if they are omitted without scandal" (Article XXVI, 41). This statement can be applied to any traditions or customs.

But when the Word of God says little or nothing or isn't completely clear, then how does the Christian decide which authorities to follow, and what is right?

Christian Liberty

295   In the city of Corinth, in the days of Paul, people believed in many gods. There were gods like Diana the huntress, Jupiter, and Apollo. Temples had been built to these gods. The Corinthians had the custom of bringing animal sacrifices to the temples to please their gods. The temple priests killed the animals and then sold the meat at very reasonable prices. The money they made went to support them and keep up the temple.

When Paul preached in Corinth many Corinthians became Christian. They no longer believed in Diana or Zeus. They now worshiped God and him alone. Many were poor people. If they could buy meat more cheaply at the temple, it would be a saving for them. Question: Was it right or wrong for them to eat this temple meat? Paul's answer is like this:

Now concerning food offered to idols: we know that "all of us possess knowledge." (We know more than these idol-worshipers; we know there are no other gods.) ... However not all possess this knowledge. (Even some new Christians are still shaky in their ideas about God and gods.) ... Take care lest this liberty of yours (to ignore the accepted meaning of old customs) somehow become a stumbling-block to the weak. For if any one sees you, a man of knowledge, at a table in an idol's temple might he not be encouraged, if his conscience is weak, to eat food offered to idols (and believe in the idols)? And so by your knowledge this weak man is destroyed, the brother for whom Christ died. ... Therefore, if food is the cause of my brother's falling, I will never eat meat, lest I cause my brother to fall. (See all of 1 Corinthians 8 and 9.)

To put it into one sentence, "All things are lawful for me, but not all things are helpful (advisable, advantageous)"—1 Corinthians 6:12.

The Christian, living in love, is above law and laws. He goes far beyond all traditions, all customs. He is a free man, free to do anything he as a Christian wants to do. He is a slave to no man and to no society. This is the freedom that Christians alone possess. Christians know what is right and wrong through the Word and love of God in the gospel. They don't need any rules or regulations. Period.   296°

Now before you go rushing off to drag race through the middle of town (which is pretty much the kind of "freedom" the Corinthians followed), remember that this idea of complete freedom applies only to Christians. The Christian is a person who loves God and his fellow man. Therefore he does not want to do anything which will hurt his brother or displease God. Or, positively, he will do all he can to help his brother and serve God. 297°

If you truly love God, love yourself, and love your neighbor, then you are free to go out and do anything you want to do, because what you want to do will be what God wants done. Your actions and your motives will be superior to all laws and customs. All things are lawful, but not all are advisable. You are a slave to no man, but a servant to all! You are free from outward restraints, but bound by your inner motives.

298° However, to whatever extent you do not truly love either God, or yourself, or your neighbor, to that extent you are still obligated to the law, and perhaps customs. Because you are still a sinner you need them. Remember, you are both sinner and saint. There is a perpetual war going on inside of you. It has been won for you, but you have not yet won it. As your inner desires increasingly agree with God's desires, you feel more and more free. Some day, through the Spirit of God, you will be a completely free person. You already hold the title to that freedom. What limits you is you.

299 The Lutheran Church, firmly believing in this idea of Christian liberty, and firmly believing that goodness starts in God and comes from within people, consistently refuses to get involved in the making of laws designed to improve morals. Some years ago many Christians believed that liquor was evil and that laws should be passed to prevent anybody from buying or selling it (prohibition). The Lutheran Church was the only major Protestant group which did not push for prohibition. We believe that you can't make people good through laws.

300 Lutherans say what they believe as individuals. They have this right and duty. But the Lutheran Church does not take an official stand for or against dancing, drinking, smoking, and most similar questions of morality. It does speak up loudly about the importance of love and faithfulness. The church, you remember, is the kingdom on the right, concerned with the gospel more than the law. The Lutheran Church is part of the total church.

Is social dancing right or wrong? How about drinking, necking, smoking, eating mashed potatoes? They are in themselves neither right nor wrong. *You* can be right or wrong, depending
301 on how and why you do them. You are moral or immoral. As a Christian you are free to do what you believe to be best. If you can love God, yourself, and your fellow man and go out and dance, drink, etc., and nobody is hurt in any way or gets into a situation he can't control in a Christian manner, then OK. You are free. The same applies to everything a Christian may be faced with doing. All things are lawful, *but. . . .*

88

At this point an additional idea needs to be added. If you have to wait until everybody comes around to an intelligent point of view, you may never be able to do anything without somebody misunderstanding or losing faith. There may be members of your catechetical class who get all shook up by some things in this book. Should it not have been written? There may be a few folks in your community who believe that all dancing is wrong. Should you refrain from dancing because they may stumble? If you do dance some will be offended; if you don't, others will be offended. In situations like these the Christian makes the most loving judgment he can and then acts. He also tries to educate the other person to his point of view.

When, in Christian love, you offend others, don't be too discouraged. Jesus once said, "Happy are those who are not offended by me." Many were. They killed him. If you want to see how love operates in real life situations, get to know Jesus.

CHRISTIAN VOCATION

God calls people to be Christians. This is their Christian call- 303° ing (vocation). God may or may not ask them to fill a specific need in society by being clergymen, doctors, ditch diggers, housewives, students, or whatever. These jobs are their occupations. Their vocation is to be Christian. This is what they are called to be. This is primary, fundamental, basic.

You are called to be a Christian. Within this framework you live your entire life. You will have various occupations, within or outside the organized church. You will have jobs, leisure time, sleep, sickness, and all sorts of things. But you are a Christian. That is your vocation.

As a Christian you have considerable responsibility. Because 304° you are one of Jesus' followers, you are automatically a leader in this world. The moment you become a Christian you have responsibilities no non-Christian has. As Jesus said, "You are the salt of the earth."

Salt gives flavor. This is your job in this world. You give it flavor. Think for a moment what that implies about your importance to society. God has called you to be a Christian in order to make society appetizing! You make it enjoyable, not by rushing around in positions of power, but simply by being a Christian. Not that you are so wonderful, but that God can work through you. You're his channel, his funnel, one of his most important contacts with other people. What a responsibility, and what a privilege! But don't forget that God has given you your saltiness. Thank God for that.

Church Occupations

305°   All occupations are equally important if they contribute to the welfare of people. Some occupations are *more obviously helpful*. It is easier to see that a doctor is helping people than a bricklayer. Both jobs need to be done. Your occupation may be that of a student. This may not seem especially glamorous, but it is a needed occupation. To a Christian being a student has the same status as being an executive. It doesn't have the same salary attached, of course, but that is a minor matter! The chances for serving God as a Christian are equally good in either job, even though not equally spectacular.

306°   Sometimes Christians seem to emphasize "church occupations" more than others. Christians should never feel that a minister, deaconess, or missionary is superior to a garbage collector, movie actor, or politician because of the job he holds.

On the other hand, the church needs ministers, deaconesses, and missionaries (sextons, organists, teachers, etc.). The Christian has a certain responsibility to see that the church's needs are cared for first. If you have the abilities necessary to do a first rate job in one of the church-related occupations, give it serious consideration. They aren't better jobs; they are jobs the church needs filled—by the right people. The church needs the very finest talent, the cream of the crop. God, who gives all talent and ability must be served with it. The church is an avenue of service.

307°   The Christian does everything "to the glory of God." Bach dedicated his music to God. A homemaker can wash dishes to

God's glory. Christians work, play, or sleep to the glory of God. That doesn't mean that everything is going to be fun or turn out profitably. It does mean that a Christian's good work will come wherever he may be. You can be in jail to the glory of God. A lot of Christians have been.

Christian Responsibility to Others

When Jesus was asked to summarize the law, he quoted two laws. He said, "You shall love the Lord your God with all your heart, and with all your soul, and with all your strength, and with all your mind; and your neighbor as yourself" (Luke 10:27).

The two go together. You can't have one without the other.

Lutherans firmly believe that each man must stand before   308*
God in a personal relationship. No one needs to come between. Each man is his own priest before God. But it is equally true that although each man stands directly before God, he never stands there alone; he is part of society, part of God's family. "*Our* Father," we pray. "If any man says, 'I love God,' and hates his brother, he is a liar," bluntly states the author of 1 John. *Brother* means anybody in God's family.

The Ten Commandments, long before Jesus' time, made this   309*
clear. The last seven commandments, and part of the third, all deal with God's concern for a good society. Jesus used some of these commandments in his Sermon on the Mount to illustrate God's demands for right human relationships.

"You have heard that it was said to the men of old, 'You shall not kill; and whoever kills shall be liable to judgment.' But I say to you that everyone who is angry with his brother shall be liable to judgment . . ."

You can see that Luther's explanations to the commandments follow Jesus' example of broadening them to include your motives, your attitudes, as well as your actions.

When someone tried to limit Jesus' summary of the law, he answered with the story of the Good Samaritan. "Neighbor" means anybody in need. The priest in the story was familiar with church traditions. The Levite (a lawyer) was familiar with

91

the laws. But the Samaritan (an outsider) knew from an inner love what was required!

There is no one living on this earth who is not your neighbor. If you ever find people on Mars or anywhere else, they will also be your neighbors. All men are in need. All men need God.

Loving Yourself

310° When people love themselves because they think they are important in their own right, they are wrong. Christians love themselves because they know that God loves them. To love others you must love yourself. Hating yourself is intolerable. Eventually you will find reasons for blaming your self-hatred on other people. Many people slowly destroy themselves by self-hatred. God's children know their worth. God has justified their existence. His way of seeing things becomes their way. It's a wonderful feeling to know that you are lovable. If God is willing to work through you, then you are definitely worth while. He did create you. He doesn't make mistakes. He also made and loves all other people. His point of view is yours.

THE FAMILY

Sentencing a person to solitary confinement is considered one of the worst punishments. Although we like to get away from people at times—and many of us should get away more often—living alone is something few people can stand for long. Man is social. He needs the company of other humans.

311 The basic social unit is the family. From the child's point of view his parents provide him with protection and the elements necessary for life while he is still too helpless to care for himself. From the parents' point of view, children provide them with a way of continuing life on earth, an opportunity for bettering civilization. For both child and parent the family provides a unit where both are understood and loved, and provides persons with whom they can share sorrows, joys, and affection.

There are all sorts of relationships within any family. God planned it that way. Only members of the same family can share the same biological make-up. (You may have noticed that even the voices of brothers and sisters have similar qualities which harmonize well.) The family unit is the cornerstone of society.

Family customs are different in various parts of the world. One north African tribe, for example, has the custom of killing off parents when they reach a certain age (around sixty). At that time it is the duty of the children to take their parents into the wilderness and leave them stranded there until they die. These people believe children have not been brought up right if they refuse to follow this custom.

In parts of China, when a stranger gives aid to any member of a family, he is then obligated to provide for the entire family (including all relatives) for the rest of their lives. You can see why social work is not popular in that area.

In Dahomey, on the west coast of Africa, the roles of men and women are reversed from our way of doing things. The women take care of agriculture, provide for the family, and fight the wars. The men raise the children, cook, and sew. Even in our western civilization there is considerable difference between the way French, German, English, and Americans, for example, raise their children or treat their parents.

The Jewish race has consistently emphasized the importance of the family unit. Christians share this attitude. They note that experiments conducted from time to time in raising children apart from parents, providing "free love" (sex relations permitted with almost anybody) for all adults, and other attempts to do away with the family unit, all eventually fail. In recent years Soviet Russia and Red China have both attempted to break up the family unit. It won't work.

The Fourth Commandment is the first of the ten which deals 312 with human relationships. It deals with the family. The sixth and the tenth also bear on family solidarity.

"Honor thy father and thy mother, that thy days may be long upon the land which the Lord thy God giveth thee." The reward attached to this law is appropriate. (Remember that blessings and curses were connected with obedience to the law.) The child who disobeys his parents is liable to get into trouble. In the rough life these Hebrews lived, failure to listen to parental advice could get you eaten by a wandering lion or lost in a canyon.

Luther's explanation of this commandment, you recall, enlarges it. He also leaves out reference to the attached reward. Christians honor their elders for a different reason. The *Table of Duties* for various people, which Luther assembled from the Bible, advises young persons to "submit yourselves unto the elder. Yes, all of you be subject one to another, and be clothed with humility . . ." It also tells parents, "You fathers, provoke not your children to anger . . ." The coin has two sides. Parents as well as children have responsibilities. Adults who are teaching young people have a way of stressing the duties of youth. It's too bad we can't find better ways of teaching parents *their* duties. The difficulty is that when they are young enough to be taught, they aren't interested in being parents. When they become parents the only ones who will listen to advice don't need it.

313°

314

Sex

315° The Sixth Commandment states, "Thou shalt not commit adultery." To adulterate something is to make it impure. To commit adultery is to make a marriage impure. Specifically this commandment forbids a married person to have sex relations (intercourse) with a person other than his or her mate. When two unmarried people have intercourse this is called having "premarital relations." Such acts contaminate the purity of subsequent marriage, and so also break the commandment.

The purpose of the Sixth Commandment is to preserve the family unit. When Jesus presented his interpretation of the law, he chose this commandment as an illustration. "You have heard that it was said, 'You shall not commit adultery.' But I say to you that everyone who looks at a woman lustfully has already committed adultery with her in his heart." Again Jesus emphasizes that the attitude is as wrong as the act.

94

Luther, typically, adds the positive angle. "We should so fear and love God as to be chaste (clean and decent) and pure (unadulterated) in our words and deeds, each one also loving and honoring his wife or her husband." You certainly do not honor your wife if you go outside the marriage to find sex relationships. A person who loves his marriage partner won't want sex outside of his marriage.

Sex is a wonderful emotion. It is part of God's plan. He created people male and female. People, normally, are happy with the arrangement. A few people, for reasons we don't yet understand, are unable to fit into this normal scheme. Instead of loving people of the opposite sex, they are emotionally attached to members of their own sex (homosexual). There are thousands of such people, perhaps millions. We need to do a lot more to understand and help these people than we do. But they are exceptions. The vast majority of people eventually become closely attached to someone of the opposite sex. The emotion of physical sex is so strong, especially when it is sudden, that many people like to think they can't control it. They can if they really want to. The problem with sex, especially for teenagers, is that it seems new, powerful, and secret. Like anything which arouses strong emotions, it can be dangerous. Wrong use of sex can, in a few minutes, completely ruin an entire lifetime. Right use brings perhaps the highest physical pleasure on earth, as well as the opportunity to have children.

In the past many religious people felt that all things of this world were evil. This is an error which is still widely held. God's world is a fine world. It includes sex. Many people forget that it was God who created us in two sexes.

Well, whether it is because they feel the world is evil, or because they believe that emotions are wrong, or because sex is so often misused, or just because they don't trust their own self-control, a lot of people feel that sex is something you do not talk about. Not getting good information, teenagers go on the information they pick up here and there. Most of this comes from slightly older teenagers who don't know the facts either. One

95

319   result is that young people are torn between two strong emotions. They feel wonderful with this emotion and the sensations that accompany it. They also feel guilty. Sex is nothing to feel guilty about. Misusing it is. Right use of it is just what God ordered.

Sex is the drive on which the family unit is based. Think of it in this way and you are OK.

320   The trouble is that our society complicates the picture by putting in other factors. For example, you are sexually mature in your teens, but in our society you are not ready to support a wife and family for several more years. Education takes longer and longer. You have to put off getting married. What shall you do with your perfectly healthy sex emotions in the meantime?

321   Some teenagers go ahead and have sex relations and hope they don't get caught or accidentally have a family. This is risky and wrong. Others substitute some form of physical self-satis-

322   faction (masturbation). Doctors state that this practice is fairly common during one stage of teen development, but the danger is that some young people get so used to this that they never grow into the more satisfactory sex life later on.

323   One problem is that our society glorifies sex. Advertising appeals to it. Dirty jokes connect physical sex with "being adult." The teenager who wants to prove he is grown up thinks he has to have physical sex contacts to do so. This is nonsense, but try to tell someone who wants to think it's true! (Anyhow, trying to prove you are grown-up only proves that you are not.)

The sex drive can be diverted into other channels which let you get rid of this energy in an acceptable way. You know that when you are seething with anger, a long walk or chopping some wood, or any other physical exercises can help you work off your hatred. In a similar way, the teenager who can occupy his mind and body with other things, will find that he can then handle his sex drives much more easily, transferring their power into other projects.

324   Another problem is that sex is a big area. It includes not only intercourse but encompasses friendships. Some folks believe that

96

the sex drive leads eventually to all noble emotions, to love of neighbor and even world brotherhood.

How much physical sex, and what kind, should a teenager 325° allow himself? Should he stop with holding hands? Is necking OK? How about petting? Perhaps even social dancing is too sexy? What about the good-night kiss? By now you know what the answer is going to be for the Christian. Act in God's kind of love—not puppy love, or sexy love, but God's love. If you can't act in love, remember the law.

The Sixth Commandment, as Christians interpret it, requires moral purity. Your body is the temple of God. It has tremendous capabilities, tremendous potentials. Through you God can work many things, even perform miracles. Your body is a gift of God. Sexual abuses always weaken the individual. Whole empires have collapsed when their moral standards decayed, when citizens felt free to do anything their passions suggested. Sex used chiefly for self-pleasure can destroy all the fine and noble qualities that God has given us.

It can also destroy the most beautiful friendships and cheapen the most wonderful love. A life that is morally sound, and sexually correct is one of the finest creations God has produced. The man who is "chaste and pure in words and deeds" is a man who can live with himself, with his neighbor, and with his God.

The family unit is so important that not only is our highest 326° idea of God, as our heavenly Father, derived from it, but both the church's sacraments are connected to it.

Baptism brings us into the Father-child relationship with God, and automatically all God's other children become our brothers and sisters. Under the law they are our neighbors. Under the gospel they are our family.

Holy Communion is a sacrament in which we share as a family our common love for God and each other: "For as we are all partakers of this one Bread and drink of this one Cup, so are we all one body in him." This family of believers (communion of saints) is even more intimate than the social family unit. When someone told Jesus that his mother and brothers were nearby,

97

he pointed to his disciples and said that these were his mother and brothers. (The Roman Catholic Church has never been able to get it through its head that Jesus has a closer relationship with his followers than he had with his earthly mother, Mary.)

Certainly we owe much to our mothers and fathers, but God is our Creator and the Father of our living selves. Our parents were his chosen agents.

Marriage and the family unit are sacred. Lutherans have stated that in the event of a divorce, both parties must accept the responsibility for it; no party is ever completely innocent. A divorce is always wrong, but sometimes it seems to be the lesser of evils. If one marriage party has committed adultery, deserted the other by walking out, or is refusing to live as husband or wife, then a divorce may be the solution. The marriage no longer exists in any true sense. Neither party can remarry unless showing evidence of repentance. This is not a law of the Lutheran Church, but it is accepted practice.

COMMUNITY

327   The next social unit after the family is the community. Usually we think of the community as a group of people in a certain geographic area, the town or section of city in which we live. For those living on a farm, the community may consist of a few homes nearby or several dozen homes spread over a large territory. For those living in city suburbs or in a small town, the boundaries are easier to establish. In a big city, however, there are likely to be several kinds of community. The person living next door may be completely unknown. Friends are chosen through business contacts, church contacts, social contacts. These people may live many miles away. We are all members of several kinds of community which may or may not be made up of the same people.

Your Communities

328   You are a member of a school community, a church community, your neighborhood, and some special groups. Each com-

98

munity has its own sets of standards, rules of conduct, rewards and punishments. In school you are rewarded and punished by the giving of grades, encouragement and discipline, based on your intellectual ability and study habits. In church you seem to be judged by your moral standards, by your faithfulness in attendance, by your general friendliness. Your neighborhood gossips about you or keeps quiet according to your way of fitting into its accepted customs. Do you get home about the same time other young people of your age do? Do you respect the property of others? Are the things you enjoy doing understandable to your neighbors? Are you active in the "important" organizations of this community? These are the things that matter. Your group judges you by your willingness to conform to its customs or your ability to lead the others. If your clothing is different, you may not be accepted. If your parents limit your activities much more than the other kids are limited, you become an outsider. If you consistently come up with ideas for good times and things to do, you are a leader.

In every community you have certain benefits, certain special privileges, and certain responsibilities. There are pressures put on you, and you put pressure on others. The amount of pressure that a group can put on one of its individuals can be tremendous. Everybody knows how easy it is for a member of a gang to be led to do things which he by himself wouldn't have nerve to do, or would not even want to do.

A group is never Christian. Individuals of the group may be; in fact all the individuals may be. But the group cannot act out of love; only its members can. So the Christian has the duty to judge by his own Christian conscience everything his groups want to do. He can never allow himself to be completely submerged in any community, not even the church.   329

The whole Jewish-Christian tradition is full of helps for Christians who, living in communities, have to decide when to go along with the group and when to stand alone. The Ten Commandments have always been regarded as a basis for conduct. Even non-Christians consider them valuable.

THE TEN COMMANDMENTS

We have already discussed many of the Commandments and Luther's explanations to them. Here are a few more ideas, some of them perhaps new to you.

Printed with the First Commandment is a paragraph which is in parentheses (see page 175). The second part of the paragraph is not so much a part of the commandment as a statement showing why God is giving his people these laws. The same thing applies to the verse which introduces the commandments, "I am the Lord your God, who brought you out of the land of Egypt, out of the house of slavery. . . ."

God had saved these people, had gathered them out of Egypt through Moses, and had guided them through the wilderness. He had a right to ask of them that they be faithful to him and obey his laws. Though God has not led us out of slavery in Egypt, he has taken us from slavery to the world, has sent Jesus to set us truly free, and is leading us through a wilderness into his promised land. He has a right to ask of us that we be faithful. He is still acutely conscious of those who hate him; and he is always filled with love for those who obey.

330   (Note that Lutherans consider the First Commandment to have two parts. Some churches make these parts into two separate commandments. Lutherans then divide the rules about coveting into two commandments, where other groups consider the Ninth and Tenth to be a single commandment.)

First Commandment

331*   We know that there is only one God and that he is sovereign. In the old days, people used to carve statues of "gods" and actually worship these. These engraved (graven) hunks of wood and stone were believed to have power and spirits in them. We no longer make graven images, but we do set up idols. Anything we place ahead of God becomes an idol which we worship. It may be money, or the affection of a friend. It may be freedom to do what we want, or acceptance by our friends. It may be community recognition, or the desire for eight hours

100

sleep a night. Almost anything can be an idol. Anything we treasure more than God, even for a moment, in that moment is our god, our idol.

What are your symbols for success? For what goals do you live? Where are your treasures? What is most important in your life at any given moment? "I am the Lord thy God. Thou shalt have no other gods before me." This is the absolute demand of God for every moment of our lives.

Second Commandment

When something is done in vain, it is empty, of no use. Taking 332° God's name in vain means to use his name for no good reason, to call on him for something that is empty. It is a supreme insult to ask someone of importance to do something useless. You know how you feel when someone calls you on the telephone and then hangs up after you say "Hello." Before you say "God damn" without intending to send someone to hell, or explode with "Jesus Christ" without beginning a sincere prayer to your Lord, remember the impression you would make on God. The impression that such loose use of God's name makes on your parents and friends is important enough, but think how God feels. How would you feel?

It isn't the use of an occasional curse word that is wrong. It is the attitude that your God is someone whom you can take lightly which is obnoxious. Few people curse with any serious thought of what the words say. They use the only way they've always heard to make a point strong. If you want to break the habit of cursing, sit down and think up a few other phrases that you can put in here and there to show how excited you are; leave abuse of God out of them.

For the Christian there is more to this commandment than not cursing. Note again what Luther says in his explanation of it: ". . . but call upon him in every time of need, and worship him with prayer, praise, and thanksgiving." The right attitude toward God and all that he stands for will lead us to a reverent use of his name, an attitude of devotion, and an eagerness to

101

be in his presence. The importance of this is emphasized by the fact that Jesus' model prayer, in the very first petition, asks God to help us to the proper attitude: "Hallowed be thy name . . ."

Third Commandment

333*   The sabbath is Saturday. The word comes from a Hebrew word meaning "rest." According to the Exodus story, the sabbath is tied in with God's resting after creating the universe; in the Deuteronomy account, it is tied in with man's need of a regular period of rest (Deuteronomy 5:15). This is clearly what Jesus had in mind when he said, "The sabbath was made for man, not man for the sabbath . . ." (Mark 2:27).

334*   Note what Luther does with this commandment. He relates it to our desire to hear God's Word, study it, and live it. The Jewish sabbath is a day of rest. The Christian Sunday is a day of worship. There is a difference, a big difference.

Sunday has been set aside by the church so Christians, in thanks for Jesus' life, death, and resurrection (on Sunday), can come together for special worship and instruction.

The question of Sunday movies in your community, what sorts of activities are permissible, how many church services, and all similar questions must be settled in the light of the Christian concept of the Lord's Day, not the Jewish idea of the sabbath. Your community has customs. Some are wise and others may be foolish. What you will do about Sunday depends on the extent that you love God, respect traditions, and can act on the basis of a Christian conscience.

Fourth Commandment

335*   Remember that Luther interprets this to include authorities in your communities. You shouldn't go your own way without gospel reasons for doing so. (Review paragraph #312.)

Fifth Commandment

336*   Jesus expanded this commandment to include nasty attitudes toward others, even those expressed by someone muttering con-
102

temptuously, "You fool." Our obligation to our neighbors is to assist and comfort—help them avoid trouble, do what we can when trouble does come, aid them in picking up the pieces afterward.

Sixth Commandment

Sex, marriage, and the raising of children are such divinely-granted privileges that we should do all we can to keep them on the highest possible level, and not foul them up with short-term or long-term selfishness. (See paragraph #315.) 337*

Seventh Commandment

You can steal a man's reputation by spreading false rumors. You can steal a man's self-respect by running him down, either to his face or behind his back. You can steal his privacy by taking too much of his time. You can steal his property by messing it up in a thousand obvious and subtle ways. The Christian helps his neighbor improve and protect his possessions. 338*

(Note that this commandment assumes a right to private property. Some nations do not grant this right.)

Eighth Commandment

This is one of the commandments frequently broken. People don't take it seriously. We delight in putting the least charitable interpretation on other people's actions. Maybe we do this because we want them on that lower level where we inwardly feel we are. This is often true of our relations with our pastor. We put him on a pedestal (where he usually doesn't want to be) and then, seeing him up there, chip away at him when we find that he is human. 339*

It is one thing to talk about a friend and correctly evaluate his abilities so that you can treat him honestly, accept him as he is, and help him to improve; it is quite another thing to tear him apart. It is false witness and malicious witness that this commandment opposes—in a word, gossip.

Ninth and Tenth Commandments

340*   Coveting is wanting something somebody else has. It does not mean wanting something like it. If your neighbor is munching on a candy bar and you would like one too, this is not coveting. If you want *his* candy bar, then you are coveting.

These commandments also assume that private property exists. (How much property any person should have, and what kinds are legitimate, are other questions. Should there be a limit on wealth? Has any state the right to take over all possessions for the common good?)

341   The Ten Commandments deal with community life as it existed in the days of Moses. Community life has changed its outward forms many times since then, but human relationships have remained the same. Perhaps they always will. The Ten Commandments are as valid today as they were over three thousand years ago. They clearly indicate God's concern for our dealings with others.

Christian Social Responsibility

342   Two things stand out in Jesus' own dealings with community life: 1. He was concerned with the people in his communities who needed help; and 2. He didn't go looking for trouble.

It is a little dangerous to see what Jesus did or didn't do and then assume that this is precisely how Christians should act today. Jesus had a different mission than we have. Our responsibilities as Christians are not identical with his responsibility as Christ. Yet there is much we can learn.

343*   Clearly he wanted his followers to be involved with the people around them. Not only did he spend much of his time healing people, helping them with their problems, teaching them the gospel, but he gave his disciples parables which indicated their responsibility to those in the communities around them.

He told a story about God's judgment, in which people are divided into two groups, "sheep" and "goats" (the goats are the butt of this parable). The basis for the division is their

104

action toward their fellow men. Jesus says that what has been done for others has been done for him; what has been left undone for others has also been left undone for him (Matthew 25:31-46). Notice the illustrations he uses in the story: feeding the hungry and thirsty, clothing the destitute, comforting the sick, visiting the prisoner—all very practical ways of helping your neighbor in your community.

When Jesus sent seventy of his disciples out on a special mission, among the things he told them to do was to heal the sick. There is also the story of the Good Samaritan, which was given as the answer to the two questions: "Who is my neighbor?" and "What must I do to inherit eternal life?"

The most important job Jesus' disciples were given was to spread his teachings. In Jesus' own work the healing and comforting and visiting were by-products of his work as teacher—which brings us to the second point.

Jesus did not go out looking for trouble. There were many 344° serious social evils in Jesus' communities. Nazareth, Jerusalem, Caesarea Philippi, and other towns needed many social reforms. Lepers were thrown out of society and not provided with adequate care. Prostitution was cruelly handled. Many courts favored the wealthy. Tax collections were a scandal. Jesus did not directly reform any of these. The nearest thing he did to undertaking this kind of social action was to throw the money-changers out of the Temple. Even this action grew more out of a religious issue than a social one.

What Jesus did do socially was to give help to every single person who asked him for help. No matter how many times he was interrupted, no matter how busy he was, nor how important his project, if anybody asked his help he gave it. There were times when he took advantage of a casual contact to extend his help to those who wanted to ask but didn't have the nerve. He did this with the woman at the well (John 4:7 ff).

Considering the fact that God sent Jesus into the world to 345 save the world and that his failure would have meant eternal death for all human beings, you might have expected him to

105

use his years on earth to scurry all over the globe frantically solving social issues, running governments, controlling education. Jesus spent about three years in active ministry. That's the time he had to solve the world's problems. He spent all that time teaching a few disciples, speaking to anybody who would come to hear him, and helping the eager people in whatever community he happened to be.

Looking back over two thousand years, would you care to disagree with his method of doing the job?

346   The point of all this for those of us who follow him is not that we shouldn't be concerned with the ills of our society, but that we *must* be concerned with any "neighbor" who needs our help. It does little good for a northern white to get legislation passed which will force southern whites to treat Negroes more fairly if he cannot be fair to the Negro family in his own community. Though a Christian gives all sorts of support to the work of missionaries in lower Slobbovia, if he neglects to help his own neighbor become a Christian, he has failed his job. Though we support the work of the church in its programs of aid to unwed mothers, sailors on leave, prison reform, care for the aged, and all its other doings, if we have not cared for the people right around us, we have done nothing.

347*   When you think of how many people you run into every day in home, school, shops, church, or just walking around, and how many of them have needs to which a Christian could speak, and then think how few you have stopped to help, it shakes you up. It should. You are responsible to God for these people.

The fact that they don't come up to you and ask for help is no excuse. You ought to be the kind of person that makes others eager to get your help. Jesus was that kind. People crowded around him. How many crowd around you?

Jesus made it clear that our first concern was the people with whom we just naturally come into contact. What we do for them, we do for God. Where we fail them, we fail God.

348*   We also have the responsibility to speak out against injustices in our communities. Jewish-Christian history is full of men who spoke out boldly. Although Jesus made no speeches directly attacking social ills, he did think highly of the Hebrew prophets. The Christian church has always considered it part of the Christian's job to improve his communities.

Being a citizen in two kingdoms, the Christian has a two-fold responsibility. As a citizen under local authorities he has the duty to help establish justice and secure domestic tranquility. As a citizen under God's Word he has the duty to act as God's interpreter of the higher way of life, lived in love.

Jesus' followers don't go off into the mountains and stay there, hiding from the world, trying to escape daily living in community. You can't be the salt of the earth as a hermit. There may be a place for monasteries, but not as an easy way out of your responsibility to live with people and be their salt and light and yeast and brother.

One of the joys of a Christian who knows that his job is 349* living where he is comes through a realization that he thereby serves God. What can you do for God who needs nothing? You can show him your love by helping others. Here is a way to respond with your whole personality, not just with mind and heart, but with every talent possessed. Here is the opportunity to do something clear and real in the battle between good and evil where it is being fought—in your life and your neighbor's.

Another joy that comes from knowing that your primary 350 responsibility is living as a Christian right where you happen to be is that you can relax a little about world problems. The dangers of Red China trying to wipe out our civilization, the narrow nationalism of newly-formed nations, the mass movement of the world's peoples toward security in place of freedom, the gradual moral decay of America, the possibility of invasion from outer space, or any other problem that you can do very little about—none of these should shake you up. So you can't change the course of history. So you can't reverse the trend of the times. So you can't avoid a nuclear world war. Don't worry about it. You *can* do the really big job God wants done, by serving your neighbor!

The devil took Jesus up into a high mountain and showed him the kingdoms of the world. He offered Jesus control of the world. Of course, to get control quickly Jesus would have had to make compromises. Jesus refused. The point of this story is that Jesus chose to live his few short years in far-off, unimportant Palestine, not as a world ruler. He didn't bother to drive out the Roman army. He didn't concern himself with the loose morals of the Greeks. He paid no particular attention to the idol worship in Babylon and Egypt. (Of course God cares about these things.) But Jesus did *his* job.

You have yours as a Christian. Maybe you will be one of those few who can get into positions where they do decide world events. Probably not. If you can, do. If you can't, that's all right. God works in his mysterious ways his wonders to perform. As a Christian you are the salt of the earth to your neighbor.

THE STATE

351   After the community, the next larger area of society is the state or nation. Some day there may be one world government, but that day is not yet here.

There are various types of state: communist, socialist, republic, totalitarian, and others. Some are definitely in favor of Christianity; some are completely opposed to it. Most don't care.

352   There is no such thing as a Christian country. There may be a country filled with Christians, or one in which the Christian church has a high position, but a country or nation cannot be Christian. It forms the other kind of kingdom. It may be just or unjust, God-fearing or indifferent, but a country cannot love; only people can.

Even the Hebrew nations of Israel and Judah, supposedly living under God's law, never achieved that goal. Prophet after prophet pointed out how far short of the law his nation fell. Amos, Hosea, Isaiah, Jeremiah, Ezekiel, and all the others tore into the abuses of justice which their governments allowed.

353°   These prophets were patriots. They loved their country so much that they were willing to face the wrath of congressional investigating committees or anybody else in order to help their

108

country improve. Every one of them was misunderstood. Some were thought to be traitors. At least one was killed. These prophets knew that the strength of the nation lay in its allegiance to God's law and that all the armies in the world could not protect it if the nation didn't do the job it was supposed to do, if it didn't provide justice and an orderly existence in which citizens could obey God.

America had a patriot who said, "My country right or wrong, but my country." If he meant that he was willing to do what was wrong if his country demanded it, then he fell short of his Christian duty. We obey God rather than man. But if he meant that as a citizen he had a duty to his country, no matter what it asked of him, then he was right. Duty to country is not always to obey it, but to do what one can to make it better. The real patriot criticizes his nation because he loves it.

You are probably more critical of the members of your family than of anybody else. This is often because you love them so much that you want them to be perfect. Love of country can express itself the same way. For the Christian it must.

In the United States, and to some extent in Canada, there is 354 a policy of separating church and state. This policy grew out of the misuse of church power by the Roman Catholics and the misuse of state power by many governments, including those where Protestants dominated.

The idea is to keep the two kingdoms from interfering with each other's jobs. The church should not try to make laws, and the government should not try to be the Christian conscience or the spreader of the gospel. This separation is splendid, but it can lead to several wrong ideas.

Separation of church and state leads many people to think 355 that the two have nothing to do with each other. This is false. Both are under God. Both have many of the same people. Life cannot be divided into what you do for the State and what you do for God. You are one person, and you simply cannot say, "Here I operate as a citizen of the state, and there I work as a citizen of the church." Our schools, for example, feel compelled

109

to keep religious education out of the classroom. Perhaps this is wise, but some of your classmates may actually think they are getting a complete education even though God's law and Word are seldom mentioned. How can you be educated if you aren't being told the purpose of life? You are being educated to make a living but are not being shown how to live.

Churches provide Sunday schools to make up what public school education lacks. One hour a week in a church school hardly compares with thirty-five spent in public or private school.

356° Another error that creeps in with the idea of separation of church and state is that the church has no right to speak out on social problems. Of course it has. So has every Christian. We not only have the right but the obligation. If the government did a perfect job of establishing justice and order there would be nothing for the church to say on this score. But the church is the prime keeper and interpreter of God's Word. It must speak out, just as the prophets did. It must not make laws, but it must proclaim the gospel.

In the past Lutherans have been guilty of considering political jobs to be inferior. There have been times when politics were corrupt. There have been times when the organized church was corrupt, too. This can still be true of both. We need Christians in political office. We need them everywhere.

God or Man

When the Christian cannot in good conscience go along with one of the mores of his community, he can ignore the custom and often get away with it. When the Christian cannot go along with a rule of the family, he may have a harder time, but can usually defy the rule and survive. But when a Christian cannot obey a law of the state, he's got a real problem.

357 He must act in the light of his conscience, doing what he believes God wants him to do. This may not be what God wants other people to do, so the Christian should be careful not to criticize others. Yet he must do what he believes is right. If 358° he lands in jail, under the law, he accepts this and lives as a

110

Christian in that situation. If obeying God rather than the state gets him killed, then he dies like a Christian. We do not mean that the Christian must passively accept all consequences. We do mean that when such circumstances come he acts as a Christian should, without bitterness, without vindictiveness, without hatred, with love and forgiveness. Witness Jesus before Pilate and on the cross.

The Lutheran Church respects your right to obey your conscience. If, for example, you believe that you cannot fight in a war (not due to fear, but because of love), the church will support your liberty to make that choice. You may go to jail, to a dirty work camp, or be shot. The church will say what it can to prevent unjust treatment, but it will not make laws to protect you. If the state laws are unfair, Christians, as citizens of the state, will have to try to change them. Meanwhile you obey God rather than man. The church will also support the right of a Christian to fight in a war if he believes this is what God wants in such a terrible situation. **359**

THE WORLD SOCIETY

The next larger area of society is world society. Some day we may discover that there is a galactic society or an interstellar social structure. Until then the earth's three billion people compose our largest group. **360**

Although the Christian church is growing in numbers, the "population explosion" which the world is going through means that Christians are becoming an ever smaller *percentage* of the people in the world. In A.D. 1960 Christians were slightly more than a third of the world's population (at least, those who called themselves Christian), but by A.D. 2000, they will probably be less than a fourth. Imagine this happening in a city! **361**

Clearly Christians have a responsibility beyond the borders of their nation. When the vast majority of people don't even know God's purpose in creating them, never heard of his law or his love, something must be done.

362°   There are concerns about justice, orderly government, social reform, and education. When earthquakes shatter, hurricanes rage, famines gnaw, and plagues destroy, the Christians of the world must step in quickly and do whatever is in their power to do. Each Christian, as tourist, missionary, government envoy, or business developer must be a Christian brother to each person he contacts, a "little Christ" to every neighbor.

363°   The primary Christian responsibility in this present world situation, however, is to spread the gospel. Another word for gospel is *evangel* (good news). Spreading the good news is called evangelism. You will note that *angel* is hiding in that word. An angel is a messenger of God.

According to Matthew's Gospel, the last words of Jesus to his disciples were in the form of a great commission (sending out), "Go therefore and make disciples of all nations, baptizing them in the name of the Father and of the Son and of the Holy Spirit, teaching them to observe all that I have commanded you; and lo, I am with you always, to the close of the age." There were only a few Christians at the end of Jesus' earthly ministry. There was a whole world to win. There is still over half a world to win. In fact, with each new generation there is again a whole world to win.

364°   If evangelism is the spreading of the gospel, then what is missions? By now you have discovered that the church uses many words which overlap with others. There are a number of ways to distinguish between the missionary work of the church and the work of evangelism.

It is the church's mission to evangelize. Anybody who is sent out (commissioned) is a missionary. His job is to evangelize, to tell the Word of God. You, as a Christian, are an evangelist wherever you are. But if you have been especially sent out, you are also a missionary. Evangelism is what the Christian does in winning to Christ the people in his communities. Missions include the work of winning and helping others in outlying areas, usually away from the self-supporting home church.

112

Lutherans believe in "the universal priesthood of believers." 365°
As we have already said, this means that each man stands
before God without the need for a pastor or priest or anybody
else to come in between. You are your own priest.

The doctrine of universal priesthood has still another meaning 366°
for Lutherans. It means that each Christian is responsible to
carry God's Word to other people, as a priest is responsible for
the spiritual welfare of his parishoners. You are a priest to all
other men and women. In North America where millions of
people are not even connected with any church, this responsibility of each Christian is perfectly clear.

Ezekiel told a story about a watchman. The watchman's job
was to stand at night at an observation post at one corner of
the city wall. If he saw an enemy approaching he was to shout
a warning so the people inside the city would wake up and get
armed. One night the watchman saw the moonlight reflected
off an enemy shield. He was sure that an enemy was readying to
attack. If he shouted a warning, the city folk might not pay
any attention. They might simply say, "Oh, he's imagining
things," and go back to sleep. Said Ezekiel, the watchman's job
is to give the warning. If he fails to give it, both the city and
he will be destroyed. If he does shout the warning, the city
still may be destroyed, but he will have done his job. Referring
to the duty of a prophet (and of a Christian), "he will have
saved his own soul."

We are the watchmen for humanity. The people you meet may
not be aware of the Enemy. It is your job to warn them. Fail,
said Ezekiel, and you both die. Warn, said Ezekiel, and you
may not be heeded, but you will have saved your own soul. The
point is clear. We Christians have a tremendous responsibility
to all men, in our family, our communities, our state, and our
world.

THE CREATION

Our Christian opportunities for service extend beyond people 367°
and include all creation. God gave us the universe. He told us

to govern it. Our responsibility to all living things and to all matter or energy includes appreciation and stewardship.

God made the universe for us. He made it good. Other people may look up at the skies at night and see only stars. To Christians the heavens are telling the glory of God and all earth shows the work of his hands. Others may look into the hearts of their friends and see only human affection. Christians see the love of God shining through the love of people. Others may look at themselves and be amazed only at the marvelous complexity of their physical bodies. Christians say, "I am the temple of God."

368*   Our responsibility to the whole of creation is to appreciate it, all of it. For us it's a friendly universe. Even if it is in the nature of all life to live at the expense of other life, nevertheless, God planned the universe. He designed it well. For his purposes it is right. It is, therefore, good for us.

369*   Our second responsibility is stewardship. A steward is a person who takes care of property. If he uses the property as his master wants it used, he is a good steward. If he allows it to become run down or wastes it, he is a poor steward. God has given us a physical world and a measure of time. We are his stewards.

A steward has to be a good person, but also a smart one. Sometimes he has to take calculated risks. He must be imaginative. For some reason many Christians have a tendency to be conservative, afraid to take chances, wary of all new ideas. This is not necessarily good stewardship. Luke 19:12-26 is a case in point. This steward played it safe. It turned out that playing it safe was really playing it wrong.

370   Too often we get the impression that stewardship applies only to the amount of money we give to the church. Money does equal time and labor, but we also must practice stewardship of natural resources, human abilities, animal life, time apart from labor, personal energy.

371*   God works for good in everything, says one Bible verse. It is a great and unending joy for you that as a Christian you are able,

114

with God's help, to take anything, any time, any situation, and bring good out of it. This is almost fantastic, but Christians, through the grace of God, can do it. Stewardship of God's universe yields tremendous satisfaction, because we are fulfilling the responsibility he has given us. (See Genesis 1:28.)

If this is my Father's world, as hymn writers suggest and we believe, then how can other hymn writers say, "Guide me, O thou great Jehovah, pilgrim through this barren land"? Because we are pilgrims. This earth, splendid though it is, is not our final home. By comparison with heaven, it is barren. Besides, there is this conflict within us. The battle still rages. There are times when we do not handle the universe correctly, or the universe does not seem good to us. Like the Hebrews wandering through the wilderness, eagerly waiting to reach the promised land of Canaan, so we wander through this life with its magnificent scenery and its daily bread, eagerly waiting for the promised world to come.

Today, nevertheless, is a day the Lord has made for us. Rejoice and be glad in it.

372°

III

MAN AND THE CHURCH

Somewhere back in the eons of unrecorded time, long after the first living cell waved farewell to its other half, a creature appeared who had the audacity to be self-conscious. He called himself *man*. The more conscious he became of himself, the less concerned he became of his Creator. Of all such men who peopled the earth, only a few were loyal to their God. Like a piece of cloth left over after the rest is used up, they were a *remnant*. 373*

Abraham was one of the remnant. He moved west from his home town of Ur into the fertile crescent. His tribe, the Hebrews, grew. In succeeding generations, under Isaac, Jacob, and Joseph, they migrated into Egypt. There a pharaoh forced them into slavery. Some grew to like Egypt, its luxury and its gods. Others, the remnant, were led out of Egypt by Moses.

In the wilderness many were unfaithful, adopted the customs of neighboring tribes, and worshiped neighboring gods. The remnant marched on; behind Joshua they conquered the land of Canaan. They established a kingdom. Solomon built a temple for his Egyptian bride, to another god. Then the kingdom split into two parts: Israel on the north, Judah on the south. Other kings allowed the worship of Baal, a Canaanite god. The prophet Elijah protested. Only a remnant joined his protest. As years passed other prophets also demanded loyalty to God. They foresaw the destruction of the nations if the people would not be faithful. Isaiah named his son "A-Remnant-Shall-Return." (It sounds better in Hebrew, but not much.) The majority were not faithful. The Assyrians conquered Israel. The Chaldeans conquered Judah.

Some Jews fled to Egypt; some were taken captive to Babylon. Years later a remnant returned to rebuild the city of Jerusalem and to worship God in a temple again.

Then the Greeks conquered Palestine. Next came the conquering Syrians, the Egyptians, the Romans. Some Jews followed Greek customs, some followed Syrian ways, some followed Egyptian customs, some followed the Roman life. Only a remnant remained loyal to God.

Then Jesus was born. Many heard his teachings. Many saw his life. A few followed. They were the new remnant. With them he established the church. He created and guided it by God's Holy Spirit.

374°

Jesus' disciples spread the church through Palestine. Paul carried it to Asia Minor, then Greece, then Rome. The church was persecuted by Nero and other Caesars. Christians fled; many compromised; some remained faithful. Slowly the faithful triumphed. The Emperor Constantine made Christianity the official religion of the empire. Eventually it became known as the Holy Roman Empire.

The early church had no carefully planned organization, but several congregations grew prominent. They were in Jerusalem, Antioch, Corinth, Alexandria, Rome, and Ephesus. Their leaders were important. The leader of an important church became known as an archbishop.

When the city of Rome was threatened by invasion from northern tribes, the capital was moved to Constantinople. The archbishops of Rome and Constantinople each gained power. The church split. The part that centered in Constantinople formed the Eastern Orthodox Churches. Rome became the head of the Western Church. Eventually the head of the church of Rome was given the title of pope (father).

The western branch of the church grew stronger and stronger in material wealth and political power. After a while it was in a position where it could dictate to kings. It did.

Meanwhile errors (heresies) were creeping into the church. Many were weeded out; other flourished. The organized church, its councils, and its pope considered itself superior to Scripture. The Virgin Mary was made increasingly prominent. Good works were considered an important part of salvation. Purgatory

118

became a place between heaven and hell. Distinctions of value were made between clergy and laymen. Law seemed more important than gospel.

Reformers began to protest errors. Some were killed. Princes of various states were now ready to rebel against church controls. Many Christians were dissatisfied with the church's official positions and its unofficial actions.

When Martin Luther asked for a return to the gospel many 375 took the opportunity to rebel. Luther himself wanted only a reformation, but the Roman Catholic Church forced a complete break. Protestantism began. The remnant of the faithful returned to the faith of the apostles.

Protestantism spread through Europe, then to America. The 376 Roman Catholic Church made a few changes, but not basic ones. (It still holds the pope to be supreme. It increasingly worships the Virgin Mary. It still emphasizes good works as a way of earning salvation, considers priests to be superior to laymen, emphasizes law above gospel, and assumes that it is the only church with the right to exist. It refuses to recognize the worth of the individual's conscience.)

Lutherans grew strong in Germany and Scandinavia. England became Episcopalian and Methodist. Switzerland and Holland were Reformed. France, Spain, Ireland, Italy remained Roman.

In America the colonies varied, depending upon where the 377 settlers came from. Lutherans settled in Pennsylvania, parts of New York, Minnesota, Michigan, and Missouri. Although many Lutherans were early settlers in Nova Scotia and Ontario, Upper Canada was officially Anglican, Lower Canada Roman Catholic.

Currently there are three major Lutheran groups in the United 378 States, *The American Lutheran Church* (ALC), the *Lutheran Church in America* (LCA), and *The Lutheran Church—Missouri Synod*. There are about seventy million Lutherans throughout the world, about nine million in North America.

From Abraham to the present has not been a long time in the history of the earth, but for man it has been an important time. In this period of history God revealed his true self. In this period of history God called a remnant and Christ established his church. In this period of history, through the church, the Word of God has come to you.

THE CHURCH

There are several definitions of the word "church." In order to avoid needless confusion it is wise to know which definition a person has in mind when he uses the term.

379°   1. Church: The one, holy, Christian Church. This is the church established by Jesus, with himself as its head. This church is universal. (Another word for universal is *catholic*.) It is made up of all true believers in God through Jesus Christ. Only God knows which persons are faithful followers and true believers. Since only God knows, we call this the *hidden* church. The Apostles' Creed uses another term, calling it the "communion of saints," the fellowship of believers.

380   2. Church: A denomination—a large number of Christians organized into a particular group. This definition places emphasis on the organization and administrative scope of the group, as well as on a particular set of beliefs. The Methodist Church, the Roman Catholic Church, the Lutheran Church are examples of this kind of church. The Lutheran Church can be subdivided into various churches (same definition), such as the *Lutheran Church in America, The Lutheran Church—Missouri Synod, the Evangelical Lutheran Church of Germany, the Lutheran Church of India*, etc. The membership of this kind of church is fixed by the official membership rolls.

381   3. Church: The individual congregation and its building. This is the basic unit of the organized church. The place where you worship on Sundays is called your church. You may be referring to the building, or to the whole unit, including the congregation which worships there. Examples: St. Mark's Evangelical Lutheran Church in Lumberton, North Carolina; Emanuel Lutheran Church, Duluth, Minnesota.

Definitions 2 and 3 refer to a *visible* church whose membership can be known from the records which are kept. The ideal

120

situation would be one in which the visible church included exactly the same people as the hidden church. Since there is no way of knowing precisely who is a true saint and who isn't, we have to make educated guesses and allow for error. Organized churches set up certain standards for membership which are intended to help separate true members from false ones. Speaking of the problem of identifying his followers, Jesus said, "By their fruits you shall know them." We are not in a position to judge people by their motives and inner allegiances. We have to decide things on the basis of appearances.

It is believed that if a person has expressed his allegiance to the Christian church and been baptized, he is a member of the hidden church. He will want to join a congregation with other believers. A congregation needs certain minimum rules 382 in order to carry on its work. The Christian who is planning to join a congregation reads the church's constitution and has its particular requirements explained to him. If he agrees to the rules and requirements he is admitted to membership in that organization. The requirements usually take the form of: (a) agreement with the Christian beliefs held by the congregation, (b) participation in the Sacrament of Holy Communion (how often varies with each congregation), (c) some financial contribution (the minimum amount is rarely specified), and sometimes (d) other general signs of interest in the church.

If a member fails to commune over a period of time, or fails 383° to make some contribution to the work of his church, it is assumed that he has lost interest. If, after a talk with the pastor or another church official he still shows no interest, he is dropped from the roll of *active* members and placed on the *inactive* list. Immediately efforts are begun to evangelize him, to win him back to the gospel.

There are a few churches here and there with such odd requirements for membership, or such poor administration, that some people find little religious value in them. Such situations are rare. The trouble with many Christians is that once they find anything they dislike about their local congregation, they are quick to leave the church rather than try to correct the fault. Martin Luther strongly protested against the errors in his church, but he tried to remain a member.

384°   There are lots of nice people outside the church. Many of them do fine deeds. It is false to assume that church members are necessarily better "good-deed-doers" than non-members. They have no corner on the ethical market. In fact, where but in the church can you find people gathering together and stating publicly that they are sinners? Christians join the church because they want the fellowship of other Christians, and they want the opportunities the church gives them to worship God together and to serve them in ways only the church can make possible. As we need to receive food regularly to live physically, so we need the regular spiritual nourishment we get in church.

Sometimes people ask why there are congregations at all. Isn't it enough to have the one, holy, Christian church? Why organize? Why form congregations and synods and denominations? The Augsburg Confession defines *church* in a way which leads to an answer:

385°   "The church is the assembly of saints *in which the Gospel is taught purely and the sacraments are administered rightly.* For the true unity of the church it is enough to agree concerning the teaching of the Gospel and the administration of the sacraments. It is not necessary that human traditions or rites and ceremonies . . . should be alike everywhere." (Article VII.)

"Our churches teach that nobody should preach publicly in the church or administer the sacraments unless he is regularly called" (Article XIV).

The church exists wherever God's Word is proclaimed correctly and the two sacraments of the church, baptism and Holy Communion are properly administered. In order to be sure these things are done intelligently, decently, and in helpful order, people must be trained. A situation must be set up to assure that God's Word is being taught, not the opinions of anybody who feels like speaking. A situation must be set up to assure that baptism and Holy Communion are handled in a refined, reverent way.

386°

122

Therefore, we have organized ourselves into churches, provided seminaries to train leaders, established congregations and synods to set standards for the conduct of pastors and members of congregations, and agreed on proper forms of worship. All organization within the church is there to protect Christians from false teachers and sloppy handling of sacred things — to see to it that the gospel is purely taught and sacraments rightly administered.

Of course, even with all the organization we have, we are still humans. Once in a while a pastor may confuse his own ideas with God's Word. Occasionally a few church leaders start pushing traditions, rites, or ceremonies as though these were essential and had to be uniform. Such abuses need correcting. It will be your duty to see to it that they are corrected. But the church remains the church.

Hundreds of years ago church members questioned whether baptism and Holy Communion are any good if administered by an evil pastor. It was decided that, "Properly speaking, the church is the assembly of saints and true believers. However, since in this life many hypocrites and evil persons are mingled with believers, it is allowable to use the sacraments even when they are administered by evil men" (Augsburg Confession, Article VIII). 387*

This is comforting. It means that God works through his church and our churches no matter how good or bad the minister and administration may be. This is also comforting to your pastor, who knows that he is human and often worries about his preaching and teaching, whether he is getting his own ideas mixed in with God's Word. Of course he is, but he doesn't have to be perfect in order to tell the congregation that Jesus said, "Be ye perfect." The pastor can speak the truth even though he cannot live up to it. No Christian can live up to it. Members of churches sometimes forget this obvious fact and often criticize their pastor for being human. You cannot expect him to be a better Christian than everybody else. But he is a specially trained person and should be a leader.

Besides its concern for Word and sacraments, the organized church, by its very nature, provides opportunities for fellowship, for worship, and for the co-operative service.

Co-operative Service

388   Jesus told his disciples to go into the whole world, baptizing and teaching. You are one of Jesus' disciples. Well?

Mormon young people, during their early twenties, give a full year to preaching their faith throughout the world. We do not demand this of our young people. It might be a good idea if we did. Few of us, though, are in the position of being able to go to other nations and preach the gospel. So instead of going ourselves, we get together with other Christians and send missionaries to these other countries in our name. They do our job. Missionaries must be carefully selected and carefully trained. Work in mission fields needs intelligent organization and thoughtful financial support. By yourself you could not tackle anything this extensive, but by banding together with other Christians in the church you can.

As a result of the co-operative work of Christians through their churches there is mission work going on in most parts of the world, so that the rest of God's earthly family can learn to know their Father.

389   Christians pool their resources in many areas to accomplish through the church what they cannot do alone. Christians in one community band together to form a congregation. The congregation, for example, can provide religious education in the form of a Sunday school, weekday schools, a vacation church school, and other agencies for the children of its members. The congregation can provide a "Pastor's Fund" which he can use to help needy members of the parish. The congregation can influence the com-

390°   munity in many ways which the individual Christian cannot.

A congregation has its limitations. So congregations in a section of the country get together to form synods. Synods handle similar jobs of training and service over a larger area. They have the responsibility of supplying vacant churches with pastors who can fill in when a pastor moves or is sick. They have responsibility for colleges and seminaries on their territory. They work with migrants, orphaned and aged, sick and imprisoned, and in many areas where an individual alone or congregations alone could not be effective.

124

Synods, too, have limitations. They, through their congrega- tions, form an even larger group, such as the *Lutheran Church in America,* or *The Lutheran Church — Missouri Synod,* or *The American Lutheran Church.* (Names of these churches are sometimes confusing, each group wanting to say in its title that it is Lutheran, a church, and in America.)

These major sub-divisions of the Lutheran Church do many kinds of work for you which you could not handle alone. They maintain standards so that all pastors will get good training, so that services of worship will be uniform enough to help you feel at home wherever you travel. They provide a co-ordinating office for the church auxiliaries such as the Luther League. They set up groups of people (Boards) responsible for American Missions, College Education and Church Vocations, Parish Education (even synods wouldn't have the manpower and money to provide books such as this one), Pensions (so your congregation needn't worry about supporting several retired pastors), Publications, Social Ministry, Theological Education (seminaries), World Missions.

Besides these boards there are also Commissions (slightly different in administrative procedures) on Church Architecture, Church Papers, Evangelism, Press–Radio–Television, Stewardship, Worship, Youth Activities, etc. Even a church court is provided in case there are matters which need that kind of settlement.

All this administration, and all the millions of dollars that are needed to make it work, are supplied to provide each individual Christian with the opportunity to serve God by serving his fellow men in larger circles and in more effective ways than would be possible if he stood alone. Some of the money you give to your church goes to the synod of which your congregation is a member and is called "apportionment." A proportion of the money that goes to synod is sent on to the larger church for its work. Without your contributions of various kinds — money, special skills in leadership, personal interest, and support — the larger church could not function.

Sometimes people feel that the organized church has grown like a mushroom during a hot, damp night. There is too much organization. Money is being wasted on office space, travel expenses, needless personnel, advertising. Why should we support all this structure? What do we get out of it — besides appeals for more money!

The trouble is that most people are not used to thinking in larger sums than their family budget. They have little conception of what it is like to have several million people working together on common projects. The moment someone mentions a thousand dollars, it seems like a huge sum. And when the church talks about millions of dollars, why, how could anyone need that much money for anything? Compared with what you are carrying around in your pocket, or with the family food money for the week, the sums the church spends are huge. But compared with the job the church needs to do in this world, compared with the ability of several million people to pool their resources, the sums are certainly in line. If anything, they are too small for the needs. Christians, too, have got to learn to think big and to act big.

The church is there to provide you, among other things, with opportunities for service that you could not have without it. The church is not infallible; it does make mistakes. When you see one, work to correct it. You will find, however, that when you compare the organized church with other organizations, it makes remarkably few serious errors and is extremely careful, though not perfect, in its stewardship of your resources.

Co-operative Worship

393°   Your church also provides you with the place, forms, and leadership for worship with other Christians. Jesus said to his disciples that where two or more of them would be gathered together he would be there with them. Through the years the churches have developed forms of worship which express the beliefs of their members. When these forms are unstructured and informal they are likely to reflect a casual or a highly emotional approach to worship. When these forms are precise and orderly

126

they probably reflect a thinking man's religion tied in with many years of historical growth. Those folks who don't care much about the heritage of the past have a freer type of service. Those who glorify the past often have a stiff and highly formal service. Those who respect the contributions of yesterday's genius as well as today's needs are likely to have a form of worship that is both dignified and expressive. Lutherans feel they belong in this category.

Each person has different needs and different ways of express-   **394***
ing himself. It is almost impossible to find one form of church worship that meets the needs of everyone's nature. Some Lutherans will always prefer a free kind of service, with emotion-laden hymns, free (made up as you go along) prayers, and an order of worship that is not tied up with the past and that may change from Sunday to Sunday, or from moment to moment. Other Lutherans, feeling insecure about the present, will retreat into the past so completely that they will be happy only in the rituals and rubrics (rules for conducting services) of long ago. The vast majority of Lutherans, however, both appreciate the thought and work of their church ancestors (men like Luther and Bach), and enjoy living in the twentieth century. *The Service,* which we use every Sunday morning, combines heritage with present needs.

There is a great advantage in using forms of worship that   **395**
have proven helpful for hundreds of years. You have the opportunity of enjoying the best that has been produced by thousands of people, and you have the assurance that you are getting a more complete approach to worship in a more durable form than you might if you based your worship on whatever appealed to you at the moment. On the other hand, if the language of the past is dead for you, and artificial respiration won't revive it, it needs to be buried and a living language put in its place.

As you go through the services and forms of worship (liturgies) of the Lutheran Church, you will find many words, phrases, and forms that seem empty. Many will take on meaning as you grow into them through study, practice, and maturity.

Like most things of great value, they cannot be appreciated all at once. There are magnificent gems of language and faith set into our forms of service. You will discover them with the passing of time and growth in experience.

You will also stumble over a few pieces of lusterless rock.

All forms of group worship provided by the church are intended to help Christians worship God together in beauty and in truth. The music of the hymns and the wording of their stanzas have been chosen to accompany each other in meter and mood. Our hymnal is outstanding among Christian hymnals. Few Lutherans appreciate the depth and beauty of our hymns. Sometime look at the lists of authors and composers (pp. 991-999). If you know poetry and music, you will recognize a lot of great names listed there.

396*

Many phrases used in the liturgy echo the Bible. Many sentences are direct quotations *The Benediction* is an example. Since the Bible is our source for knowing Christ, the wording of our liturgies reflects our respect for Scripture.

397*

The Introits, Collects, Lessons, Epistles, Graduals, and Gospels (pages 75ff) have been chosen to fit into a yearly plan, called the Church Year. These *propers* (proper for the occasion) have been selected to give each Sunday service a smooth flow (the Gradual, for example, helps you go from the thought of the Epistle "gradually" into the thought of the Gospel), and to give the whole year of church services a rounded approach to Christian faith and life. All this is done to help you worship with other Christians in the most complete and beautiful way.

398
399

There are typical questions people often ask about our worship:

1. How is Easter dated? (First Sunday after the first full moon after the 21st of March.)

2. Where do those Latin words come from in the names of the Sundays after Easter? (From the first words of the Introits.)

3. Why do we use the Nicene Creed instead of the Apostles' Creed when we are having Holy Communion? (It is a more complete statement in regard to the person of Christ and the person

128

of the Holy Spirit, both statements being especially appropriate to Holy Communion.)

4. Why do most Lutherans stand for prayer, while Methodists sit? (Custom. Lutherans show respect by standing.)

5. What determines when the minister faces the altar and when he faces the congregation? (The nature of what he is saying or doing. Is he leading the congregation in speaking to God or is he bringing the people a message from God?)

As you participate in Lutheran worship services, make a list 400 of questions which you would like to have answered. Our customs, rituals, traditions will mean more if you understand them.

The Service

The service of public worship which we use every Sunday is 401 carefully constructed. All parts fit into place neatly. There are a number of ways to illustrate its pattern. One of the better ways is to compare it with the Christian's life.

The Christian's life begins with a relationship to God. *The Service* begins with the announcement that this service is related to God, and asks his presence (Invocation). The Christian, living in relation to God, realizes that he is a sinner. He confesses his sinful nature. He asks God's forgiveness. God forgives him when he is sincere. The opening part of *The Service* is called the Office (assigned place) of Confession. The minister, speaking for God, declares God's forgiveness.

In the Christian life, the forgiven sinner can now enter into God's presence as a new man. The Service follows with the Introit (entering). At this point the action follows the thought. Now, for the first time, the pastor, representing the congregation, goes past the altar rail, up to the altar, the focal point for the presence of God.

The natural reaction of the new man in Christ is to praise God for his love and forgiveness and to ask his continual help. The Gloria Patri, Kyrie, Gloria in Excelsis, and Collect express these feelings. The Collect also leads into the next part of the service.

129

After the Christian has praised God for his love and forgiveness, he wants to know more about God. The lesson from the Old Testament, the Epistles, the story of Jesus in the Gospels, together with the sermon, make up the Office of Instruction.

Hearing the Word of God, and being a member of Jesus' church, the Christian states his faith for all to hear (Creed), and prays for the church and for all mankind (Prayer of the Church).

At this point he offers God his self (Offertory), his possessions (Offering), his prayers.

402* (The Service is designed to continue on to its climax in the Holy Communion, but is often ended at this point by the Benediction.)

In the intimate fellowship of the saints (believers), the Christian prepares for the sacrament of Holy Communion, also called the Eucharist, or the Lord's Supper.

The believer's thoughts are directed to God (Preface). The command of Christ to use this Sacrament is read (Words of Institution), often in a prayer (Prayer of Thanksgiving), and the elements (bread and wine) are set apart (consecrated) for this act.

The Christian, using his physical senses of sight and touch and taste, comes into fellowship with his Lord and with all other Christians.

Having been lifted into the presence of God, and having shared this sacred experience with his fellow Christians, the Christian gives thanks, and returns to serve God in his daily life.

So you see, the Christian life is reflected, re-enacted, embodied in our chief form of public worship. Every Sunday Christians come together to praise God for their lives: their sinful selves, God's forgiveness, his love, the new life, their communion with him and with others. No wonder that this service is considered one of the highest forms of worship.

403 The church has built up other forms of worship. Morning worship is called Matins (morning) and evening worship is called Vespers (evening), both words coming to us from the Latin by way of the French.

130

For special occasions there are special forms of service. Pages 404
242 to 273 of the *Service Book and Hymnal* include the ones used
most frequently. Your pastor has a little book with many others
in it.

THE SACRAMENTS

Among the benefits which God gives Christians through the
church, the two sacraments are outstanding. God has chosen to
put these into the hands of the church. They do not exist apart
from it. They are two more reasons why the Christian will want
to belong to a congregation and be active in it.

A number of things go into making a sacrament. First of all, a 405
sacrament is an act of God. The thing that makes it a sacrament
is what God does. We may worship in the sacrament, but God is
the agent. A sacrament also comes as the direct result of God's 406*
command to have it. This is not a ritual which the church has
dreamed up. God said, "Do this." And a sacrament also carries 407*
with it certain specific promises from God. The whole gospel is
focused in a sacrament. We know that God does not withhold
himself from anyone who wants his help. In a sacrament, though,
we have a situation in which God has clearly laid down the form
through which his gift is given.

A sacrament is under the authority of the church. Christ has 408
put it there. The church gives it or withholds it. This does not
means that a particular church can arbitrarily prevent a person
from becoming Christian or keep him from fellowship with God
and other Christians (as the Roman Catholic Church states), but
it does mean that these two sure signs of God's grace come
within the framework of the church.

Finally, the sacraments make use of "earthly elements." In 409*
Baptism it is water; in Holy Communion the earthly elements are
bread and wine. These physical things are means through which
God's Word is made tangible and concrete to us. By itself the
water is an excellent symbol for the washing and cleansing of
baptism, and the bread and wine are symbols of the body and
blood of Christ. But because they are being used in a special
way to convey God's Word, they become more than symbols.

131

Precisely what they become is impossible to explain. They don't change into something different. Nor can you think of them as you would of the red corpuscles in your blood stream, each one carrying food or oxygen with it; a little bit of God's presence doesn't come along with every little bit of wafer or wine. Something other than this is involved. It is the combination of earthly element with the Word of God that makes the sacrament what it is.

Baptism

410   Almost all societies have initiation rites. Fraternities and sororities take people into membership through various rituals, sometimes humorous, sometimes serious. Primitive tribes have rituals associated with the change from childhood into manhood or womanhood. In many places it is customary for a boy of thirteen to be given a hunting knife and taken out into a remote area of the jungle. He is left there alone and must protect himself against wild animals, find his own food, and after several days return to his home unassisted. When he succeeds he is accepted as a man. For several days he is then "king of the roost" and celebrations are given in his honor. If he fails, he is buried.

In one part of Europe, several centuries ago, teenage boys were placed into a deep pit. Over it was spread a network of boughs and branches. A bull was led to the center of the branches and killed there. The boy was bathed with the blood of the bull. By this he was initiated into the tribe.

We still have a few related customs in society today. Debutantes have "coming out" parties. Social fraternities have initiations. The church has confirmation to mark a Christian's "coming of age" in his responsible relationship to God. The church has baptism as its initiation ceremony.

411   Baptism is a fine example of how the church has taken traditions and rituals of pagan (non-Christian) origin and transformed them into something vastly superior. You might say that the church takes the forms and materials of this world and redeems (rescues and fulfills) them. The church takes customs that

132

are tinged with meaning and dyes them with full-color truth. Most social traditions and religious rituals are based on some understanding of man in relation to a higher power. The Christian church, possessing the revelation of God in Jesus, takes these partially filled glasses and pours them full. In many cases the containers need only slight modification.

It would be foolish to put a round truth in a square ritual. **412** The church must guard against adapting customs that are not compatible with its beliefs (for example, taking the pagan symbols of fertility, such as eggs and rabbits, and tying them with the "new life" of the resurrection). On the other hand, many things common to the experience of all humans are also valid and valuable within the church.

That Baptism existed before the time of Jesus is clear from the fact that John the Baptist was practicing this rite before his cousin Jesus began to work. Baptism, as John used it, was a ceremony which indicated a person was starting afresh — washing off his past sins and evil ways.

When Jesus came to be baptized by John, the Baptist couldn't **413*** understand how a sinless person like Jesus could need baptism. But baptism also was a rite of initiation or entrance, a rite of dedication. Jesus allowed himself to be baptized not because he was a sinner, but because he was to take *our* sins and was dedicating himself publicly to a special relationship with God.

The Bible account of Jesus' baptism says that he was baptized **414*** "in" the Jordan River. Mark relates that after his baptism he "came up out of the water." The Baptist Church believes that these passages indicate that Jesus must have been immersed (plunged into) in the river in order to emerge from it (come out of). Therefore Baptists *insist* that a person must go under the water in order to be baptized. But the Bible isn't explicit whether Jesus stood in the water or was submerged during the ceremony. Lutherans think it doesn't make any difference whether a person is immersed or has water poured or sprinkled on him. Neither do most other Christian groups. We use pouring and sprinkling because it is more practical.

415°   In the early days of Christianity it often happened that a whole family was baptized at the same time. If the father became Christian, it was assumed that the rest of the family followed suit. Religion was a family affair. So it became the custom to baptize children. Again, the Baptists disagree with this procedure. They, and some others, believe that only adults may be baptized, for only adults can be responsible for their own faith, have the maturity to accept or reject Christ. Other Christians don't see it this way. We reason that since it is God who makes faith possible through his Holy Spirit, and since we always have the freedom to reject him, why not baptize children? This sacrament gives assurance of a child's relationship with God and in no way limits his freedom to reject God if he later should choose to.

Suppose that both parents of a baby are involved in a fatal accident. Suppose, too, that some wonderful person wants to adopt this baby. Should we wait until the baby is a teenager before the adoption is offered to him? Should the baby be deprived of love and care and a family just so that later on he can decide for himself — when it's too late — whether the love and care and a family would have been desirable? When you are a parent, will you wait with your children's education until they are old enough to decide whether or not they want it?

Christians want their children to have all good things. Supreme among these is God's adoption of them as members of his church family. In baptism we have the *stated assurance* that anyone who believes and is baptized will be saved. It does not say that baptism and belief must coincide in time. An adult can believe first and be baptized later. A child can be baptized first and come to believe later. Of course, for a normal adult to be baptized without believing would be a mockery of the sacrament. An infant, though, is not in a position to believe in God, or if he does, cannot communicate this to the rest of us.

416°   Since there is nothing magical about the Sacrament of Baptism, we realize that a child who is baptized must have the Word of God taught to him by other Christians before he can assume personal responsibility for his faith (at confirmation). Therefore

134

Lutherans stress the importance of Christian sponsors for the child. They bring him to be baptized. If the parents are Christian, they are usually the sponsors. They are in the best position to bring the child up in a Christian way, and confront him with the Word of God. However, baptism is a church sacrament; the whole church is responsible for this child's growth as a Christian.

Some adults get excited when they hear the pastor say, "Almighty God, the Father of our Lord Jesus Christ, who hath begotten thee again (created you as a father does) of water and the Holy Ghost, and have forgiven thee all thy sin, ..." They reason that this infant was just born a few weeks ago, so how dare the church say that their darling has committed any sins? What the church is saying is that this child is a human being, by nature sinful. Being part of the human race that has already separated itself from God, the child shares this separation and needs to be forgiven and accepted. It is this that God does in baptism, forgiving sin and granting life and salvation. No man can divorce himself from his human heritage, whether he wants to or not. The question of willful disobedience to God may not be a factor in the life of the infant as yet. It will be as time goes by. **417***

This initiatory rite of the church is a sacrament because it is something which God does, because God commanded it, because God promises certain benefits through it (forgiveness of sins, deliverance from death and the devil, and everlasting salvation), and because an earthly element is included. The water in itself does nothing. It is easy for people to attribute power to the water itself, to think that the water may be kept and used to get rid of warts or something. People do come up with the craziest superstitious ideas. If you will look at Luther's explanation of baptism in his Small Catechism, you'll note that he gives a fairly long answer to the question, "How can water produce such great effects?" His answer is clear and straight to the point, as usual. "It is not the water indeed that produces these effects, but the Word of God which accompanies and is connected with the water, and our faith, which relies on the Word of God connected with the water. . . ." **418**

135

419   Luther's words, "accompanies and is connected," point up one of the intellectual difficulties many people have in appreciating the sacraments: the connection between the Word of God and the earthly elements. As we said (marginal reference 409 e.g.) these earthly elements are means through which God's Word is made tangible and concrete for us. So "the water, without the Word of God, is simply water and no baptism. But when connected with the Word of God, it is a baptism. . . ." The water is more than a convenient marker informing us that something historical once happened here, or a sign announcing a present event. Just as God once put his Word into the form of a human being (Jesus), and just as our love is expressed to others through the specific forms of action we take, so God's act of forgiveness and adoption in this sacrament are tied in with the forms of the sacrament, the words spoken and the water used.

420*   The water is also a symbol of washing. In baptism we are cleansed. Luther uses the symbol of water in a similar way by saying that "it signifies that the old Adam in us is to be drowned . . .; and that again the new man should daily come forth. . . ." The idea of drowning and rising out of the water comes from the event of the Hebrews crossing the Red Sea. The Hebrews considered this rescue from the Egyptian army to be a focal point of their entire history. Their story is the story of a people lost from God, whom he constantly rescued. So Paul refers to the Christian baptism as a similar type of event, in which God rescues us. Luther emphasizes that this is really a daily occurrence in our lives; we are constantly in need of rescue, of a daily baptism. The sacrament does not need to be repeated, but we do need God's Holy Spirit to "daily forgive abundantly all my sins . . ." We are baptized of water and the Spirit.

        The Sacrament of Baptism is more than a ceremony announcing our relationship with the church and our dedication to Christ.
421*   It unites us with Christ in a way we cannot fully understand. We are, you may remember, baptized *into* Christ. There is a union of each Christian with Christ. When God adopts us as children in his church family, there is immediately a relationship

136

so complete that the normal ties of family members don't quite illustrate it. To use an earthly expression, we are of one blood. We are related as branches are to a vine, as parts of a body are related to each other and to the head, as . . . But no earthly illustration suffices. We therefore say that Christ dwells in us and we in him, and hope someday to understand mentally what we now know only in faith.

At the time of confirmation we accept responsibility for the promises made by our sponsors. God's baptism of us remains valid whether we confirm it or not. Only if we wilfully, completely, and persistently reject God can his work in us be undone.

What happens to people who die unbaptized? We aren't sure. 422° The Roman Catholic Church believes that people who have never heard of Christian baptism have a separate place set up for them, popularly called Limbo. Other Christians don't believe this and feel that God alone is in a position to know what the situation requires. He is always loving, even to those who do not know it. God will do what is good for the person who has not heard the gospel and for the unbaptized child. We know what happens to the person who is baptized and does believe. He is saved.

Holy Communion

Almost all societies have fellowship rites. Sometimes people 423 stand in a circle, cross arms, and hold hands. This is known as a fellowship circle and is sometimes used at camps. Meals are considered a form of family fellowship. Americans traditionally consider the Thanksgiving dinner to be a special time of family communion (sharing together). All over the world, and since the times of the earliest peoples, being invited to eat at someone's table, to share his meal, has been considered an act of acceptance and close association.

The Last Supper that Jesus had with his disciples before his 424° death became a very special event. The Jews were celebrating the feast of the Passover, remembering the time when the angel of the Lord passed over the homes of the Hebrews in Egypt and God delivered them from the slavery of the pharaoh by killing

137

every Egyptian's oldest son. God saved the Hebrews from slavery by the shedding of blood.

A few hours after this Last Supper, God was again going to save his people by the shedding of blood. Jesus would be crucified. He knew what would happen, that he would have to die, that through his death and resurrection people could be saved from death. The man who follows Christ shares in this experience, and follows him through death into new life.

425°   Now, in this evening hour, in an upper room somewhere in Jerusalem, Jesus was having the last meal with his friends. They could not yet understand how they would become part of him and he part of them. This intimacy of fellowship was as yet beyond their comprehension. But Jesus understood. And so he "took bread; and when he had given thanks, he brake it, and gave it to his disciples, and said, 'Take, eat; this is my body, which is given for you; this do in remembrance of me.' After the same manner also he took the cup, when he had supped, gave thanks, and gave it to them, saying, 'Drink ye all of it; this cup is the new testament in my blood, which is shed for you, for the remission of sins; this do, as oft as ye drink it, in remembrance of me.' "

426   Here again is an act of God, the remission (sending away) of sins, commanded by Christ ("this do"), using earthly elements (bread and wine), and given through the church (made up of close disciples) with his promise (forgiveness and communion with Christ). This is the second sacrament.

427°   It wasn't until after Jesus' resurrection that the first disciples began to realize the significance of the Holy Communion ceremony. Then they understood. When he had said, "This is my body" and "This is my blood" he had meant the bread and wine to be more than a symbol. They were meant to convey this union. Eating and drinking has always been connected with possession. "I could eat you up," we say when we like someone.

Of course we don't eat Christ's bodily flesh and drink his physical blood like cannibals, but he is truly present in this sacrament; there is a sacred fellowship, a holy communion.

138

As the disciples were in intimate fellowship with each other and with Jesus at that Last Supper, so we are in the same intimate fellowship with other disciples and with him whenever we take part in (partake of) this sacrament.

The belief that Jesus Christ is actually present in his glorified body is called the doctrine of the Real Presence. We worship a living Christ, living *in* us, *with* us, and *under* our entire existence. He is a real part of us — yet not cell by cell. In this sacrament he comes "in, with, and under" the elements of bread and wine — yet not cell by cell. This is a mystery. 428°

Of course the presence of God is real at all times and in all places, but the sacrament focuses this reality in a concrete fashion so that disciples can grasp it more tangibly. God does not withhold himself from those who desire him. He is our everpresent help in trouble or in happiness. The sacraments, however, bring a special emphasis, a special focus to his presence.

Not only does the Christian commune with God in this sacrament, but the fellowship extends sideways to all other Christians as well. The disciples in that upper room somewhere in Jerusalem experienced something in common that held them together from that time on. That night, though they didn't fully understand it, they shared the gift of life as God alone can give it. Knowledge that they had this in common, through Christ, brought them into a life fellowship, a living communion. 429°

When you go to the altar to take Holy Communion, whether you fully understand it or not, you are in a position to receive God's gift of everlasting life. You share this with all other Christians. This is a fellowship infinitely more precious than any other on earth. Because it is the fellowship of those who share life, it even goes beyond this life on earth.

When Paul died, he was a Christian. United with the living Christ, he shares eternal life. So Paul is not dead, but living. Of course he is not living the same physical existence which we are now living, but he is alive in the kingdom of heaven. Although we cannot locate him geographically or in the realm of our kind of time, nevertheless he is alive. So is Mary Magdalene; 430°

139

and Mary the mother of Jesus—if she believed in her son as the Christ. So are Peter, James, John, and the others. So are Luther, St. Francis, your Christian great-grandparents, and you. When you take Holy Communion, you have true fellowship with all of them. This is not the sharing of a memory; this is the sharing of life with living people. This is a most glorious mystery. This is one of the heights of Christian experience. "Therefore with angels and archangels, and with all the company of heaven, we laud and magnify" our God, evermore praising him (Preface to Communion Service).

Note in the Communion hymns how vividly this idea of sharing a living fellowship permeates the words.

"One bread, one cup, one body, we,
    United by our life in thee." (265, stanza 3)

"Be still, my soul, for God is near,
    The great High Priest is with thee now!
The Lord of Life himself is here,
    Before whose face the angels bow." (267, stanza 1)

"With our sainted ones in glory (those who have died)
    Seated at our Father's board, (table)
May the Church that waiteth for thee
    Keep love's tie unbroken, Lord." (282, stanza 3)

431   As some folks have believed that the water in baptism has some magical quality, so others have felt that the bread and wine of Holy Communion carry the power of the Sacrament. Speaking of the forgiveness of sins and the gift of salvation and life received through this Sacrament, Luther answers those who feel that bodily eating and drinking alone produce such benefits. "The eating and drinking, indeed, do not produce them, but the words which stand here . . . He who believes these words, has that which they declare and set forth. . . ." "The words: 'for you,' require truly believing hearts."

140

Again, it is the Word of God which makes the Sacrament effective.

People are rarely content to let a mystery remain a mystery. They have to find explanations. Two major churches differ from the view we have outlined above. They are the Roman Catholic Church and the churches of the Reformed tradition.

The Roman Catholics believe that Jesus' Atonement is to be performed over and over again through the Sacrament, which they call the mass. They believe that the priest is the agent for the miracle of the mass, and that Christ actually dies and rises again every time the mass is celebrated. Roman Catholics also believe that the bread and wine actually turn into Jesus' real body and real blood, and that the people who eat the bread are actually eating Jesus' body. (Only the priest is allowed to drink the wine.) The belief that the elements are changed into body and blood is called the doctrine of transubstantiation. **432**

The churches which follow strictly the teachings of Zwingli and Calvin, on the other extreme, believe that the Sacrament is only a memorial, a rite performed in remembrance of the Lord's supper with his disciples. **433**

Zwingli and Luther met one time to try to iron out their differences on this subject. The language Jesus used when he said, "This is my body" and "This is my blood" doesn't require or contain the word "is" the way English requires it. Zwingli felt that Jesus' statement, "This do, in remembrance of me," was all that mattered. Luther wrote in German on the table around which the two were sitting, "This is my body." He underlined the "is" three times! You'll note that the words the Lutheran minister uses when he distributes the bread and wine solve the problem of translation, very neatly: "The body of Christ, given for thee. The blood of Christ, shed for thee." **434**

This Sacrament can be such a tremendous experience that Christians like to prepare for it as thoroughly as possible. People who feel that spiritual things and physical things don't get along well together like to discipline their bodies and appetites. They try to master their physical sensations in order to perceive the **435**

141

spiritual more fully. Fasting is often used as a preparation. People who fast during Lent are restricting the physical to emphasize the spiritual.

Other Christians do not believe that the physical and spiritual are incompatible.

436*   The important thing is to come to the service of Communion ready to receive the Sacrament, eager to confess your sin (and perhaps your sins), anxious to be in the close presence of God, and desirous of fellowship with all other Christians. (Remember that "all other Christians" includes people of all races, of all ages, with differing customs, clothing, attitudes, and habits of living. These are your brothers and sisters in Christ. With such as these you will share the kingdom of heaven. With them you now share a holy communion.)

437   There are many ways in which the Sacrament is administered. There may be one common cup out of which each communicant drinks; there may be individual glasses. They may be filled before the service or poured full at the altar rail. The bread may be put in your hand or in your mouth. You may stand or kneel at the altar, or walk by slowly. The minister may wear a blue suit, a black gown, a cassock and surplice, or a chasuble.

The details do not matter. They should add to the meaning, though, and not subtract from it. The heart of the Sacrament is the Word of God. All customs and rites and traditions should help make this Word clear, never obscure it. As far as Lutherans are concerned, it is God's revelation to us that matters, his act that counts. The externals connected with the sacrament should be neat and orderly and in good taste, but it should always be remembered that it is Christ's body and blood which strengthen and preserve. It is he whom we love and worship.

LUTHERANS, LUTHER, AND CHRIST

438   You are involved in a catechetical course. The word "catechetical," by the way, comes from a Greek word meaning "to teach orally," usually by question and answer. (You mean you got this far without looking it up?)

142

Luther's *Small Catechism*, you have observed, uses the question-and-answer approach to education. Whether your pastor is using the same technique is up to him. Currently other methods of education seem to be more popular.

Frequently we have been quoting Luther's answers to various 439 questions. Some folks—non-Lutherans of course—have accused us of worshiping Luther rather than Christ. While nobody who knows us could possibly come to that conclusion, the relationship between Luther's teachings and Christ's is important.

Luther and his friend Philip Melanchthon wrote a number of papers and books in which they stated what they believed and what they opposed. A number of these are so clear and obviously in line with the teachings of the early church, the writings of Paul, and the gospel accounts of Jesus' teachings that we Luth- 440 erans accept them as valid. Chief among these works of Luther, Melanchthon, and others, are Luther's Small Catechism and the Augsburg Confession. That these are in agreement with the biblical accounts is believed by all Lutherans. Most Lutherans would add a few others: Luther's Large Catechism, the three Creeds (Apostles', Nicene, Athanasian), the Apology (defense) of the Augsburg Confession, the Formula of Concord, and the Smalcald Articles. All these documents together form the Book of Concord. We consider these to be historically essential and presently important because they agree with Bible accounts.

Luther said a number of things which make today's socially 441 proper folks shudder. He lived in a rough and tumble era of history. Things which sounded OK then sound crude to our more refined culture. Some of his language was as rugged as he was. Luther, being human, made his share of mistakes. Since he was an important person, his students wrote down many of the casual conversations he had with them after class, in the local tavern. (The local tavern was a nice place in those days, not like many of the saloons you see on TV westerns.) We Lutherans do not agree with everything Luther said or did. He was a product of his times as much as we are of ours.

143

Luther did have a genius, though, for clearing trails through the forest of false ideas which had accumulated, for tearing out the underbrush which fifteen hundred years of history had fertilized within the church, for erecting unmistakable signposts along the one path which led where people needed to go, and for personally leading the safari to its destination.

Luther did the church a tremendous service by rediscovering the gospel and pointing it out to the church.

442* Luther did not want a denomination named after him. The name Lutheran originated with his enemies, just as the name *Christian* came from enemies of the early church. When Lutherans select a name for one of their church bodies, they often add the word *Evangelical,* to emphasize that it is the gospel (*evangel*) which is being preached not Luther.

443 Martin Luther grew up within the Roman Catholic Church. He was a good Catholic and obeyed his church carefully. When he found no relief for his inner conflicts through the practices of his church he searched the writings of the church fathers, such as Augustine. Then he read the Bible for himself (Bibles were rare in those days). Paul's interpretation of Jesus struck Luther as being remarkably different from what he had been taught within the Roman Catholic Church. He compared Paul's ideas with those of Jesus. He found that the two agreed. Paul correctly understood Jesus. Roman Catholic church leaders were out in left field. Surely this was a horrible accident! Luther believed that if he would call this to their attention they would return to the right view. So Luther nailed 95 theses for debate on the door of the church in Wittenberg (a common practice). Sometime later a staunch Catholic named John Eck debated them with Luther. It became clear that the official church would not reform. It didn't want to. The Roman Church cared more about the opinions of its leaders than it did about Paul, or even Jesus Christ. Luther had no choice; he broke from the official church. The Reformation (of the Christian church) began.

444 We Lutherans agree with Luther's major points. We see, as he did, that Paul correctly understood Jesus. We further see

144

that Luther correctly understood both what Jesus taught and what Paul interpreted. We also disagree with the customs and ideas which Luther found to be wrong. So we are Lutherans.

Paul is important to Christians because he was the first great 445° Christian who applied Jesus' teachings to congregational life. He also is important because he was probably the first Christian who understood the significance of Jesus as the Christ. Jesus' immediate disciples were a little too close to him to be objective. They didn't bother to put all the pieces together, for they were too excited about the physical presence of their Lord. Paul was more nearly in the situation we are in. He never actually walked and talked with Jesus. But he lived and taught at the time when people who had walked and talked with Jesus were still living. They regarded Paul highly. In fact, during the first years of establishing the church, he was more of a leader than Peter or any of the others. The New Testament clearly indicates this. Peter was one of Jesus' best disciples, but shortly after the experience of Pentecost, Paul took the leadership and established congregations throughout the Roman empire.

A good illustration of the relationship between Lutherans, 446 Luther, Paul, and Jesus is the use of the doctrine of justification by faith. This cornerstone of the Lutheran Church originates in the life and teaching of Jesus, who, although he never mentions the doctrine by name, clearly shows that a person's faith is what matters. Paul points out that Jesus' whole life and mission indicates that the New Covenant is based on salvation by grace through faith. Luther holds fast to this and rejects the Roman Catholic notion that works aid in man's salvation. The Lutheran Church still carefully preserves this essential part of the gospel.

There are a lot of details you need to know about your con- 447 gregation, its customs, its requirements, its benefits for you. One thing you can be sure of: if your church is Lutheran it emphasizes the Word of God. "For his is the kingdom, and the power, and the glory." The Lutheran Church is part of the larger church, the church of Jesus Christ.

448   Groups of Christians who feel differently about some aspects of faith or life have formed other churches. The major, long-established groups are usually called *denominations*. Smaller groups, nearer the fringes of Christian thinking, or outside of it entirely, are usually called *sects*.

449   Most Christians would feel more comfortable if there could be only one group, encompassing all Christians, and known as the Christian Church. However, the fact is that different people see things in different ways. Some folks prefer one custom to another. Some folks emphasize one idea above another. People who have been brought up by a strict father may feel more comfortable in a strict church. People strongly attached to their mother may prefer a church which emphasizes the mother of Jesus. People who feel unsure of themselves may want a church that has supreme confidence in itself and tells them exactly what to do. People who are confident in their own abilities may join a church which gives them freedom. And so on.

This need not imply that the many denominations came into being because people wanted to make a church to suit their wishes—although this sometimes happened. It does mean that many times people saw in the life and teachings of Jesus those specific ideas for which they were looking, and that people are still most comfortable in a denomination which holds a point of view similar to their own.

You know how a person who is against drinking will hunt for all the passages in the Bible which forbid strong liquor, and ignore verses like "use a little wine for the sake of your stomach." Roman Catholics will point with great enthusiasm to verses which emphasize the importance of Jesus' mother, or the leadership of Peter. They brush aside other passages in the Bible which tell how casually Jesus treated his mother. Lutherans hold up Romans and Galatians as outstanding books of the New Testament because the doctrine of justification by faith is clearly presented there. But Lutherans would like to agree with Luther, who once said that the Epistle of James was "a letter of straw." It states that "a man is justified by works and not by faith alone."

146

Within the major Christian denominations there is complete 450*
agreement that Christ is the head of the church, that his Gospel
is the way to salvation. The disagreements mostly lie in the
amount of emphasis one idea is to receive above another. Occasionally there is more fundamental disagreement. Even Lutherans cannot always agree with each other on such matters as
whether the Bible means exactly what it says, word for word,
comma for comma, or whether it can be interpreted correctly
only in the light of the times in which it was written. For
example, do we have to believe that a large fish really swallowed
Jonah, or was this simply a wonderful adventure story written
to make a true point, namely, that God loves all people? Even
within your own congregation not all members would agree on
that one.

Many denominational differences seem trivial to us, but other 451*
people think these specific differences are vital. Some of the
things we think are vital may seem like hair-splitting to others.

Whether you are justified by faith alone or by faith and
works . . . who cares? Hair splitting? People who fail to see
any significant difference between these points of view should
take a look at the differences which exist in the two churches
that represent these two viewpoints, the Roman Catholic and
the Lutheran. Almost all Roman Catholic custom and theology
(science of God) reflect the idea that good works help to save.
The Lutheran Church's customs and theology indicate right
down the line that it believes in justification by faith alone. Purgatory, confession, the place of the clergy, the status of the pope,
the veneration of Mary, the significance of the mass, and many
other Roman Catholic concepts are all related to their belief
that good works help to save. The importance of the Word of
God, the place of preaching, the idea of Christian liberty, the
priesthood of all believers, the worth of the individual and his
conscience, and many other Lutheran concepts are all related to
our basic belief that man is saved by God's grace and cannot
save himself.

It seems silly to start separate denominations because some prefer a church without organ music, or others think the minister should wear a certain costume. But it does not seem silly to start a separate denomination over beliefs.

Perhaps some day the visible church will be the same as the hidden. Perhaps some day denominations and sects will disappear from the face of the earth. But for the present it is not **452°** desirable, because unity would have to come over the dead body of faith. Compromise of beliefs is not wise, and for the **453°** honest man is impossible. Some people like to think they can take the best of every religion and make a super-religion from these choice tidbits. The trouble is that they throw out everythink that won't fit neatly into their scheme. The "best" becomes the superficial. Instead of ending up with a full course meal, they end up with a collection of garbage.

454 Other folks say happily, "The differences don't matter; we're all going to the same place anyway." Oh? Since when is getting to heaven the point of our religion? Doing what God wants is the point of religion. Those who are in it for what they can get out of it, have missed the point, and missed the boat too.

455 Lutherans are happy that they usually manage to tolerate— and sometimes even appreciate—differences of custom within their own group. We have highly ritualistic congregations and casual ones, too. We have ministers who wear a plain suit for the Sunday service, and others who wear about all the vestments they can find. We serve Communion by using a common cup or by using individual glasses, using grape juice or wine (mostly wine). We baptize by pouring and sprinkling but see nothing wrong with immersion. All customs and rituals, habits and preferences are allowed, as long as they do not interfere with the **456** right proclaiming of the Word and the proper administration of the sacraments. The Word of God—as we understand it— is not to be tampered with. The sacraments dare never be rearranged to suit our pet desires, to protect our sensibilities, to gratify our ambitions. God's Word is our law and our gospel. We obey, whether it suits us or not, and then love, because we

148

discover it suits us perfectly. We do these things within our denomination because we were baptized into it, because we have gotten used to it, because it speaks to our experience, because we believe it most rightly agrees with Jesus and the Father he reveals to us.

Other Christians feel the same way about their denominations. **457** They should. If they don't, they should find the denomination in which they have most confidence. So should you.

Lutherans or not, we Christians are members of the one holy Christian church, the communion of saints. This is what matters.

MILITANT AND TRIUMPHANT

The church's one foundation is Jesus Christ, her Lord. She is his new creation, by baptism and the Word. From heaven he came and created her to be his holy bride. With his own blood he bought her, and for her life he died. Her members are called from every nation; yet are united throughout the earth. Her charter of salvation is: one Lord, one faith, and one new birth in baptism. She serves one God, partakes in Holy Communion the same bread and wine. And to one hope—the kingdom of God—she presses with every power that God has given her.

Christians, who are still waging the war against evil within themselves and their church, still battling against the evil in the world, are called the *church militant,* the fighting church. **458*** "Onward Christian soldiers, marching as to war," we sing. "Christians leagued together to battle for the right." "A mighty fortress is our God, a bulwark never failing. Still our ancient foe seeks to work us harm. On earth is not his equal. Christ Jesus it is, from age to age the same; he must win the battle."

We belong to a fighting church, led by a fighting Lord, (tramping out the vintage where the grapes of wrath are stored) whose truth goes marching on. We are out to conquer evil with good, conquer Devil with God. Let there be no sleeping on the watch-towers; let all citizens of the kingdom be armed; let every soul be awake, stretching every nerve, pressing on with vigor.

149

Love is not passive. Goodness is not sissified. "Happy are the meek," said Jesus, "for they shall inherit the earth." The word meek has changed its meaning in recent years. It used to mean leadable, tractable—like the chariot horses of Ben Hur, firey, dynamic, powerful, but responsive to the reins of the driver. Happy are the firey, dynamic, powerful Christians, responsive to the reign of God, for they shall win the earth.

Your church, the Christian church, is a fighting church. It has been since its beginning, is now, and shall be until victory is complete. And it shall win. "Though this world, with devils filled," says Luther, shall "threaten to undo us; we will not fear, for God hath willed his truth to triumph through us." "Solid joys and lasting treasure none but Zion's children know."

459*   The church, the communion of saints, is dear to Christians. In it we share a profound fellowship. Its baptism assures us of life and God's adoption of us as his sons and heirs. It nourishes our faith, as a mother does her children. In it we are confirmed, married, and with its final benediction are buried.

Through our lives we come to its altars, confess our failure, unburden our hearts. Throughout our lives, before its altars we receive forgiveness from our Creator, strength to go out into the world to serve again. When we are weak, the church is a tower of strength. When we are lonely, the church is our source of love. When we are discouraged, the church is our success. When our consciences falter, the church provides guidance. When our sights are set low or when our eyes are dim, the church provides visions of new horizons and clear insight. When our hearts are heavy and our burdens unbearable, the church is a sanctuary for rest and a fellowship of burden-sharing people.

And when we are happy, our joy finds expression in hymns of praise. When our cups are overflowing, our hearts filled to the brim, our souls exuberant, then the church rejoices with us. For they that serve the Lord renew their strength, walk without fainting, run without wearying, fly like eagles.

We love the church. For her our tears fall, our prayers ascend. To her our cares and toils are given until cares and toils shall end. Beyond our highest joys we prize her heavenly ways, her sweet communion, her solemn vows, her hymns of love and praise. We love our church, and with her look forward to the time when her warfare will be over, and Jesus in his glory shall usher in the new heaven and the new earth; when the kingdom shall have come; when Christ is crowned with all crowns; when all dwellers of time and space shall bow down before him; when peace shall fling its heavenly splendors over all the earth; when we shall see the Lord in eternal rays of resurrection light and hear him, calm and plain, say to us, "All hail"; when we, in triumphant gladness shall raise the victory song.

We work and we pray for the time when our church's longing eyes are blest with that glorious vision, and the great church victorious, shall be the church at rest.

Those who have already run the race of life and crossed the finish line, those who have fought the good fight, those who have had the crown of righteousness pressed upon their brows, are in the *church triumphant*. 460*

What happens to time when people die, we do not know. It may be that they experience God's loving judgment immediately. Or it may be, as some Christians believe, that there is a period much like sleep, through which they wait until the one final judgment of the quick (living) and the dead. Paul talks about the dead "sleeping." The New Testament church clearly thought in terms of a last day of judgment, when the sheep and the goats would be separated. But hymn writers and others have also given us a fairly consistent picture of Christians who have died as living now with God. We who are still bound by time, must think in terms of future judgment. In any case, Christians are alive; the church militant and the church triumphant are one church, united in mystic communion.

The time will surely come for all Christians when the armies of the ransomed saints will complete their fight with death and sin, when God shall fling wide the golden gates, and let the victors in.

Meanwhile, the church fights on to total victory.

CANTEC ΛΟΥΤΗΘ

ΔΕΔΕΖΑΜΕΝΙ

ΥΜΜΝ ΚΑΤΑΤΟΠ

ΕΜΟΙΑΛΕ Η

ICE

ΤΟΥΚ

ΑΛΗΙ

IV

AIDS TO FAITH

"When a man is newly married, he shall not go out with the army . . . ; he shall be free at home for one year, to be happy with his wife . . ." (Deuteronomy 24:5).

"Any woman who prays . . . with her head unveiled dishonors her head—it is the same as if her head were shaven . . ." (1 Corinthians 11:5).

These are two of the many customs mentioned in the Bible. **461** Some make little sense for today's society; others still have considerable meaning. The laws recorded in Deuteronomy, for example, were made for the Children of Israel in a situation different from ours. Many such laws and regulations are completely ignored today, for example, Deuteronomy 21:18-21. On the other hand, regulations such as the one in Deuteronomy 22:5 still have some weight, and 24:16 still is the rule.

The Bible is full of all sorts of material. Between its covers **462** you can find miracles (Mark 1:40ff), great poetry (Psalms 24:7ff), tactics of warfare (Judges 20:29ff), and love songs (Song of Solomon 5:10ff). Although the line "Your hair is like a flock of goats, moving down the slopes of Gilead" (Song of Solomon 6:5) would make the modern man reach for a bottle of hair tonic, you've got to admit it's imaginative.

The Bible contains high objectives (Matthew 5:38ff), fascinating stories (Judges 15:1-8; Matthew 13:1ff), serious drama (Job 1:6-11), eternal truths (Proverbs 14:34; 11:22), religious philosophy (Ecclesiastes 1:2-7; John 1:1ff), and accounts of many of the world's most amazing personalities, such as Moses, David, Jesus, Peter, Paul.

There is so much material in the Bible, and it is so varied in **463** nature, that many folks are overwhelmed by it and don't know how to read or interpret it. People like things clear and uncomplicated; they want to know whether the Bible is true or false, good or bad. Can you live by it, or can't you? Any answer that isn't a simple "yes" or "no" leaves them uneasy.

464   The fact is that no simple answers are possible, for the Bible is not a simple book. Between its covers is found the entire history of a people, a race, a nation. Thousands of years of events, stories, philosophies, law, and interpretations are compressed into the Old and New Testaments. There is legend and truth, the commonplace and rich treasures, thoughts of man and Word of God. Sixty-six books are contained within it, and it includes collections of court records, ballads, letters, and laws. Almost every book has been rewritten, and sections have been edited over and over again. Parts have been added to earlier writings, and in some instances parts have been lost (1 Samuel 13:1). In the process of copying and recopying the manuscripts the scribes have accidentally repeated lines (Leviticus 20:10), left out letters (Psalms 2:12), and made mistakes in quoting references (Mark 1:2 is a quotation from Malachi 3:1, not from Isaiah.)

Some Bible writers were brilliant men, and some were average. Some were literary giants, and some were linguistic pygmies. Some were highly technical, and some purely imaginative. Some were accurate, and some indifferent to facts. Some were ageless in their outlook, and some reflected only their own times.

465*   Different sections of the Bible were written for different peoples (as with Paul's letters). You would write a different sort of letter to your sweetheart than to a cousin or to your teacher. You would write in a different way if you expected your letter to be read in church than if you expected it to be read privately. If you were persecuted and your letters were to be censored, you would write differently than if you were a court scribe making official records of a king's reign. All these varieties of situations are found in the Bible manuscripts.

Add to these facts the realization that the Hebrews did not regard history in the same way that we do, that they used different forms of thought, had a different conception of time, and related much of their writing to the specific situations of their

154

day, which often were quite different from ours, and you begin to see how difficult it is to understand all of the Bible. It takes work, study, thought. The Bible was never put together to be read from beginning to end. Its stories were not written for children. Much of the thinking presented in it is quite difficult.

To read the Bible intelligently you need at least a Bible dictionary, a good commentary, and perhaps an atlas. With study the Bible becomes fascinating, full of wonderful people, full of amazing stories, romance, action, and a reverence for God that is contagious. A very important point in Bible reading is to read slowly and with imagination. 466* 467*

We moderns are used to consuming huge quantities of words in order to find an idea or story. In the Bible a full length novel may be told in a few verses. The rest is up to your imagination. In many ways those early writers were smarter than us. They expected their readers to do some thinking, too. 468

All the beauty of the Bible, magnificent as it is, is incidental to the major purpose and highest value of the book, for the Bible shows us God's love. Here is the account of God's dealings with a people. Here is a running analysis of the relationship of the Hebrew race to the almighty Creator. Here, in the Bible, is the true story of God's self-revelation to all men, through patriarchs, judges, kings, prophets, and Christ. 469*

For when the time was ripe, God sent his Son to the Jews, to be born in one of their cities, of one of their women, and to grow up within their social system, to teach their people first, and to die with their screams of condemnation pounding in his ears. It was also from these people that the first disciples were chosen and the core of the church was formed. 470

The Bible contains the answers to all questions of faith and questions of a moral nature that you will meet during your life. Admittedly, you can't always turn to such and such a page to find out whether or not you should cheat in your next school exam, but between the Bible's covers lies the answer. 471

A lot of books contain answers to problems. Confucius and Karl Marx have some answers. So do many others, good and bad. The unique thing about the Bible, however, is that it contains the right answers.

The answers are not all simple. Many are quite complex. As we mature in thinking and in Bible reading we frequently discover that the arguments and problems we think are new were discussed and answered thousands of years ago. The answers found in the Bible are often just what we are looking for.

The book of Job, for example, speaks to the problem of suffering and the question whether God is just. It gives basic answers. Thousands who don't know their Bibles well enough search for answers every day. Many never find them. But there they are.

472* The main reason for studying the Bible is to learn from it what God wants of you. Since through it you can learn to accept his love and fulfill the purpose for which you were given life, and thereby have eternal life, the Bible is the most valuable thing you possess. It will help you to keep your very precious

473 life. The truth you need is presented between Genesis 1 and Revelation 22. But that's a lot of material. Some people, finding it difficult in spots, give up entirely. How should a Christian read the Bible?

Somebody once told a parable about a love letter. Suppose you were madly in love. (Is there any other way of being in love?) Your lover sent you a letter. In it were several little requests—little things he or she wanted you to do, such as answer the letter, pass on some information to the family, and some requests which you didn't quite understand on first reading. On reading the letter a second time you still couldn't quite make out all that you were to do.

Question: What would you do if you really loved the writer of the letter? Would you (1) refuse to follow any of the requests until you had deciphered all of them—even if it took years? Or (2) would you first carry out the requests you did understand and then tackle the ones you didn't?

We wouldn't think much of a person's love if that person insisted on analyzing, pondering, arguing over a few obscure

156

passages before he was willing to act on the many perfectly clear passages. We would think even less of a person who would throw away the whole letter because a few lines weren't plain. So with the Bible, God's love letter to you!

The Inspired Word

Most peoples believe in some form of God. Most people have books they consider to be sacred writings. There is, for example, the *Koran* of the Mohammedans. Why do Christians consider the Bible to be superior?

Because God himself influenced the writing of the Bible. The Bible is part of God's plan to show all men what he is like and what he wants. He had a hand in it.

The Lutheran Church believes that the Holy Scriptures are   474°
"the norm for the faith and life of the Church. The Holy Scriptures are the divinely inspired record of God's redemptive act in Christ, for which the Old Testament prepared the way and which the New Testament proclaims. . . . God still speaks through the Holy Scriptures and realizes his redemptive purpose generation after generation" (Article II, Section 3, Constitution of the Lutheran Church in America).

Lutherans believe that God *inspired* the Bible account. With   475°
this word another mystery confronts us. What do we mean by the word "inspired"? We do not mean, for example, that when Moses was up on Mt. Sinai a hand of fire roared down from heaven and with a white-hot fore-finger etched the Ten Commandments on slabs of rock.

We see that the Bible contains more than the thinking of men and women. There are insights revealed in the Bible that man, by himself, could not dream up. There are truths conveyed by the Bible that God planned, not man. The life and teaching of Jesus Christ are a life and teaching that God gave us directly.

The Bible writers were inspired men, that is, they were affected by God. They stood in his presence and knew it. They watched history develop and saw God's hand moving it.

Every comma in your translation is not necessarily accurately placed. Every incident in the biblical account is not necessarily historically true. Every concept of the universe is not necessarily scientifically correct. Every law, every custom, every point of view expressed, is not necessarily valid for our day.

476* *The Bible is the Word of God in essential matters of faith and life.* Old Hebrew science is something else again. Early tribal medicine was pretty primitive. Jewish geography was often inaccurate. The moral standards of the Israelites were not always exemplary. King David sometimes lied. Samson was immoral. Judas betrayed Jesus. Some of the writers of Genesis included stories that would shock the Boston city fathers.

But when it comes to an understanding of God, an understanding of man as God's creation, an understanding of Jesus Christ as the Savior, an understanding of the Holy Spirit, and an understanding of the church, the Bible is absolute authority. It is accurate, true for everybody.

477 There are at least three different ways to approach the Bible material. We should approach geography, medicine, history and similar subjects from a good scholarly point of view. Have we learned more science since then? Has medical knowledge advanced? Fine. Use modern knowledge and insights.

478 We should approach the personal relationships mentioned in the Bible, and similar topics, from a comparative point of view. Do these agree with our own experiences? Are people still basically the same? How are they different? New customs may fit our times better, new laws may be needed for the atomic age. Fine. Use modern experience and insights.

479 We should approach the divine-human relationships mentioned in the Bible, the truths about God, the facts beyond human experience, the interpretations beyond human wisdom, and related material, in faith. This area of the Bible is beyond our evaluations. We accept or reject it on authority we trust.

The authority for Christians is Christ. He is the most complete revelation that humans can experience. What he is, is real. What he says, is true.

158

Christians have got to know Christ. Knowing him, they can
then go to any part of the Bible or to the whole of it and recognize what is revealed and what is not, what is essential for
faith and life and what is nonessential. Christ is the heart of the
Bible.

Our primary job is to get to know Jesus Christ. Our best way
of getting to know him is through the Bible, through the Old
Testament which prepares the way and through the New Testament which proclaims him.

"We praise thee for the radiance
    That from the hallowed page,
    A lantern to our footsteps,
    Shines on from age to age.

"It is the golden casket
    Where gems of truth are stored;
    It is the heaven-drawn picture
    Of Christ, the living Word."

THE CONFESSIONS

Some people read into the Bible what they would like to see
there, and see in it what they would like to believe it says.
People who begin with prejudices, no matter how learned or
brilliant these people may be, usually manage to find passages
that seem to agree with their prejudices and fail to notice the
passages that disagree. That is why we Lutherans insist on
checking our consciences with the teachings of Jesus and the
main witness of the church.

When the church was still young there was no Bible as we
now have it. The church leaders had not yet agreed on what
writings should be included in the New Testament and what
writing should be left out. A number of writings were circu-
lated around the Mediterranean area which had doubtful author-
ship, and worse yet, contained stories about Jesus and ideas
concerning his teachings which sounded more like fiction than

159

truth and more like personal prejudices than the Word of God. Eventually, through the leadership of Athanasius, a group of writings was agreed on and it became the *canon* of the New Testament. Even as late as the time of Luther, though, there still was some question whether some books should be dropped from the canon, and others, like Paul's letter to the Laodicians, should be added. (Roman Catholic Bibles have a few books in them that Protestants have not included.)

481

482*
While trying to decide which books to include, the early church leaders agreed on certain principles for selection. Any writing would have to agree with the ideas set forth in the four Gospels, would have to be sponsored by a leading church, and would have to be *apostolic,* that is, must either have been written by one of Jesus' apostles or obviously reflect their views, for after all, these people knew Jesus best.

483
The chief reason for all this excitement about the writings to be included in the canon, was that some leaders were going around preaching strange ideas and stating that Christian writings agreed with them. As the church decided that these men were teaching false doctrine they were declared heretics.

Some heretics had interesting ideas which seemed to make sense to newcomers to Christianity. The ideas of heretics usually appeal to personal desires. For example, one group of heretics, known as *Gnostics,* spread the idea that God had given them a special revelation. They claimed knowledge above that of other leaders, secret information. Naturally this made them feel superior. They were wrong, of course, but hard to convince. (We have lots of gnostics today, too.)

One heretic, Marcion, taught that there were two gods, an Old Testament god, and Jesus Christ, who was young and superior. Some heretics said that Jesus was a human whom God had adopted as his son. Others said that Jesus was never really human, hadn't actually suffered, died, and been buried. And so on. The early church, in order to fight these heretics, not only agreed on a Bible canon, but made statements of faith which stated what Christians did believe, in opposition to heretics.

160

Apostles' Creed

"I believe in God the Father Almighty, Maker of heaven and earth. And in Jesus Christ, his only Son, our Lord" (this took care of Marcion's two gods); "who was conceived by the Holy Ghost, born of the Virgin Mary; suffered under Pontius Pilate, was crucified, dead, and buried" (shooting holes into the claims of those who said Jesus wasn't really human); "he descended into hell, the third day he rose again from the dead; he ascended into heaven, and sitteth on the right hand of God. . . ." (refuting those who claimed that Jesus wasn't really divine). 484

At their baptism, adult Christians would state the creed (belief) of the church, to show that they were aligning themselves with the true Christian faith and didn't hold to heretical ideas. Eventually a series of statements became fixed and popular. It was known as the Apostles' Creed. Although no apostles had written or used it, this creed did contain ideas which the apostles had taught, and in a general way it summarized the essential truths of the Christian faith.

Even though Marcion and his ideas are no longer around today, other odd ideas keep coming up. Many are repetitions of early heresies. So the church still uses the Apostles' Creed as its 485 basic statement of beliefs. It is used during the Sunday service, at baptisms, in the confirmation service, and at other important times. A notable exception is the use of another creed, the Nicene, in connection with services of Holy Communion.

Nicene Creed

In A.D. 325, in the town of Nice, a number of church fathers 486 assembled to settle a controversy concerning the relationship between Jesus and the Father. Additions were made to the Apostles' Creed which, in the course of time, were modified into what is now our Nicene (named after the town) Creed.

"I believe in one God, the Father Almighty, Maker of heaven and earth, and of all things visible and invisible.

"And in one Lord Jesus Christ, the only-begotten Son of God, begotten of the Father before all worlds" (Christ always existed). "God of God, Light of Light, Very God of Very God" (true God, not a special human), "begotten, not made, being of one substance with the Father . . ." (not a creation of God's, but of the very nature of God).

"And I believe in the Holy Ghost, the Lord and Giver of Life" (the person of God who keeps life going), "who proceedeth" (not created or begotten but a sort of natural extension) "from the Father and the Son . . ." ("and the Son" was put in by the Western Churches, the Eastern Churches feeling that the Holy Spirit came only from the Father-person of God). "And I believe one holy Christian (or "catholic" with a small "c") and apostolic church" (founded on the teachings of the apostles). "I acknowledge one baptism for the remission of sins . . ." (no need for repeated baptism, nor is there any validity in other forms of initiation, borrowed from neighboring religions).

487   Holy Communion brings us into a conscious closeness with the real presence of Christ. It is therefore good for the Christian to be clear about Christ's relationship with the Father. The Nicene Creed states this more fully than the Apostles' Creed. That is why this creed is used in Holy Communion.

Athanasian Creed

488   Athanasius did not write the Athanasian Creed. However, he was a great churchman and a stronger leader against the heretics who tried to change the doctrines of the Trinity and the Incarnation (marginal #103). This creed makes firm statements on both subjects. Perhaps that is a reason why it bears his name.

The Athanasian Creed is a good example of what happens when you try to put a mystery into words:

"This is the true Christian faith, that we worship one God in three persons and three persons in one God without confusing the persons or dividing the divine substance" (so far, clear and precise). "For the Father is one person, the Son is another, and the Holy Spirit is still another, but there is one Godhead of the Father and of the Son and of the Holy Spirit, equal in glory and coequal in majesty" (Still with us?).

162

"What the Father is, that is the Son and that is the Holy Spirit: the Father is uncreated, the Son is uncreated, the Holy Spirit is uncreated; the Father is unlimited, the Son is unlimited, the Holy Spirit is unlimited" (how can three persons be distinct yet unlimited?); "the Father is eternal, the Son is eternal, the Holy Spirit is eternal; and yet there are not three eternals but one eternal. . . ."

We have quoted about one quarter of the creed. You can see how carefully it is worded. This was necessary to explain the true Christian position in opposition to the learned men who taught other ideas. Many people fail to see that these differences in wording really are important. Slightly different words reflect different ways of thinking, and ultimately different ways of living. The whole truth of the gospel can get twisted beyond recognition by the substitution of different ideas about God and Christ and man. These false ideas can turn up in statements of belief as apparently minor differences in wording.

When we read the Athanasian Creed, or some of the statements made by Luther's friend Melanchthon, we might ask, "What was all the fuss about?" It's a good thing somebody bothered to "fuss" or we wouldn't have had the Reformation and might still be worshiping God falsely, still not knowing his love. If you ever run into an intelligent Communist, you may find out for yourself the importance of the right word in an argument, and what happens when you feed a fuzzy definition to a smooth heretic.

The Augsburg Confession

Besides the three creeds, Lutherans have writings which tra-   490
ditionally state the viewpoint of the Lutheran Church, especially in relation to the false teachings against which Luther
protested and the opposition of other groups to the Lutheran
position.

A statement of belief made in defense of one's position is   491
called an *apology*. This does not imply guilt. It indicates that
the statement is persuasive rather than blunt. A *confession* is   492

a statement which puts forth one's position in clear, logical order. It grows out of a historical situation, and can be either creedal or apologetic.

In A.D. 1530, Emperor Charles V called together various leaders to decide all sorts of military, political, and religious matters. Philip Melanchthon, with Luther's approval, worked up a series of statements which were intended to set forth the Lutheran position on a number of religious questions. Most of these questions were being hotly argued. All the princes and many 493 other important leaders of the German Empire met in the town of Augsburg. On June 25 the final document was officially read. During the next years it became a sort of rallying point for the Lutheran Church, which sometimes is known as the Church of the Augsburg Confession.

The document summarizes our position concerning the way of salvation and justification by faith alone. It speaks firmly about the universal priesthood of believers. It also makes several important statements about the relationships of Christians to civil authority. These statements are important enough to make the Augsburg Confession one of the basic writings of the Lutheran Church.

Other Lutheran confessional statements are:

494 *The Apology of the Augsburg Confession.* After the Augsburg Confession had been read to the assembly in Augsburg, the Roman Catholics prepared a statement which they believed showed its errors. In answer to their statement, Melanchthon prepared a defense of his original confession, known as the Apology of the Augsburg Confession. It is a long document, a valuable commentary by Melanchthon on his earlier writing.

495 *The Smalcald Articles.* During the early years of the Reformation Luther was asked to prepare a series of statements which would point out where some agreements between churches might be reached, and where he felt no agreement could be reached. His statements, or articles, were presented at the town of Smalcald. They deal with the Trinity, Christ and faith, Saints, Monasteries, the Pope, Sin, Penitence, Confession, etc.

164

The Formula of Concord. After Luther's death some of his followers split with followers of Melanchthon. In an effort to get these two groups of Lutherans together again a special document was drawn up. The hope was that both sides could agree to its formulation of the Lutheran position. This formula of agreement (concord) makes such statements as "We believe, teach, and confess that the prophetic and apostolic writings of the Old and New Testaments are the only rule and norm according to which all doctrines and teachers alike must be appraised and judged. . . ."

The Large Catechism. Luther wrote this catechism because he saw how few people actually knew very much about their Christian faith. Even the pastors paid far too little attention to learning and teaching fundamentals. Luther, in typical down-to-earth language comments:

"Many regard the Catechism as a simple, silly teaching which they can absorb and master at one reading. After reading it once they toss the book into a corner as if they are ashamed to read it again. Indeed, even among the nobility there are some louts and skinflints who declare that we can do without pastors and preachers from now on because we have everything in books and can learn it all by ourselves. So they blithely let parishes fall into decay, and brazenly allow both pastors and preachers to suffer distress and hunger. . . .

"Every morning, and whenever else I have time, I read and recite word for word the Lord's Prayer, the Ten Commandments, the Creed, the Psalms, etc. I must still read and study the Catechism daily, yet I cannot master it as I wish, but must remain a child and pupil of the Catechism, and I do it gladly. . . .

"Therefore, I beg these lazy-bellies and presumptuous saints, for God's sake, to get it into their heads that they are not really and truly such learned and great doctors as they think. . . ."

Luther's Large Catechism deals with the same subjects as the Small Catechism. The explanations, however, are more detailed.

Luther also prepared, as you are well aware, a Small Catechism for use by families. The three creeds, the two catechisms, and the four other confessional statements which we have dis-
497 cussed form the *Book of Concord*, a collection of Lutheran confessional statements originally adopted by various civic leaders of Germany, shortly after Luther's death.

The Small Catechism

498 Many members of congregations in Luther's day knew very little about their Christian faith. This was partly due to the fact that these people had not been educated in their religion while in the Roman Catholic Church, and partly because, like the Corinthians, many leaders of the Reformation had latched on to the idea of Christian freedom without taking seriously their Christian responsibilities.

In his Preface to the Small Catechism Luther described the situation: "The deplorable conditions which I recently encountered when I was a visitor constrained me to prepare this brief and simple catechism or statement of Christian teaching. Good God, what wretchedness I beheld! The common people, especially those who live in the country, have no knowledge whatever of Christian teaching, and unfortunately many pastors are quite incompetent and unfitted for teaching. Although the people are supposed to be Christian, are baptized, and receive the holy sacrament, they do not know the Lord's Prayer, the Creed, or the Ten Commandments, they live as if they were pigs and irrational beasts, and now that the Gospel has been restored they have mastered the fine art of abusing liberty.

"If any refuse to receive your instructions, tell them that they deny Christ and are no Christians. They should not be admitted to the sacrament, be accepted as sponsors in Baptism, or be allowed to participate in any Christian privileges."

499 Luther's plan for the Small Catechism grows out of the experience of the church. He selected the most important truths of the Christian faith and life. Here he describes the Catechism:
166

"The Catechism is the true Bible of the laymen, made up of the contents of Christian doctrine, which every Christian needs to know for his salvation. Just as the Song of Solomon is called a Song of Songs (a song above all other songs), so the Ten Commandments are a doctrine of doctrines (a doctrine above all doctrines), in which God's will is made known, what God requires of us, and what we lack. . . . The Creed . . . is a history of histories (a history above all histories), or the greatest history of all, in which we see the miraculous working of the majesty of God from the beginnings to eternity. . . . The Lord's Prayer is a prayer of prayers (the highest prayer of all). . . . The sacraments are ceremonies of ceremonies (the very highest ceremonies), which God himself has instituted and established, and in which he assures us of his grace."

The Small Catechism of Martin Luther received wide acceptance immediately. All the churches of the Augsburg Confession also accepted the Catechism. Because of its simple language and clear statements, all in complete agreement with the witness of the Bible, it has become one of the Lutheran Church's best known and best loved confessions. It has been said that no 500 book except the Bible itself has been so widely distributed as Luther's Catechism. It has been translated into every major world language, and into many minor ones. New translations of it are constantly appearing. It is studied from Greenland to Africa, from China to Europe. Not only do Lutherans study it, but other Protestants have used it as the basis for religious education. It is the basis for this book, too.

Try, sometime, to write an explanation to the Ten Commandments, the Creed, or any of the five parts of the Catechism in as clear and short a series of statements as Luther did. He performed an essential service to the church, and did it masterfully.

The authority of the Small Catechism is the same as that of all 501 Christian teaching: the fact that it witnesses to the truth first made clear and still most clear in Jesus Christ.

The authority of the Catechism is not Luther. It is Christ.

V

THE CHOICE

"The following persons, having been instructed in the Christian   502
Faith and approved by the Church, are now presented for the
Rite of Confirmation." After your pastor speaks these words he
will call the names of those to be confirmed. You may be among
them. Or you may not. The choice of whether you are confirmed
or not depends almost entirely on you. It isn't often that a pastor
or church council refuses confirmation to a member of a class. If
you don't want to be confirmed, you will probably have to be the
person to say so.

It would certainly not be an easy thing to tell your pastor,   503
"I'm not ready for confirmation." Your parents are counting on
your confirmation, your friends expect it, most classmates take
it for granted. There will not be many who will understand if
you choose to say, "Not yet."

It should be an equally serious decision to say, "I am ready."
Taking personal responsibility for being a Christian is the most
serious obligation any human can assume.

The introductory paragraphs of this book contain three questions which you were urged to ask yourself as you studied:

Does this apply to me?

If it does, do I want to follow it?

If I do, how will my life be changed?

If you have been asking these questions and searching for their
answers, you know by now that the Christian way of life is vastly
different from all other ways of life. God has called you to be
a Christian. Regardless of various pressures on you, you have the
choice to follow his way or go another. You have reached a
moment of decision. You either say "Yes" or you say "No." It may
be that you will want to change your decision at some future
time, but at this moment your choice must be as honest and
complete as you are able to make it.

If the pastor calls your name and you stand at the altar with the others who have been instructed, the pastor will ask you five questions. They are phrased in the traditional language of the church. The first four are very short. The questions and the answers to them will take you less than a couple of minutes to run through. The marriage service lasts only a few minutes, too. So does the funeral service. The men who signed the "Declaration of Independence" took only a moment to put their signatures on the document. When Moses read the Covenant to the Children of Israel it didn't take them long to state their acceptance of it, nor did it require much time for an angry mob to shout "Crucify him."

504°   "Do you renounce the devil, and all his works, and all his ways?" Everything that is evil in the world, in society, and in you personally—do you renounce it? Your desire to do what you want to do when you want to do it, even if it hurts others—do you renounce it? Your natural tendency to put yourself first in your own thinking—do you renounce it? When you are tempted to do anything wrong, or when a mean idea sneaks into your mind, or when strong emotions try to overcome your standard of right—are you prepared to say, "I renounce them"?

505   "Do you believe in God the Father Almighty?" By now you know that this doesn't mean that you believe there is a God, but that you recognize him as your Creator, the source of all creation, the one whose Word rules your life.

506   "Do you believe in Jesus Christ?" Not just that he once lived, but that he is your Lord, your Master, the One whom you go to in trouble and joy, the One whom you follow, serve, and love with all your heart, mind, body, and soul?

507   "Do you believe in the Holy Ghost?" The giver of life, the person of God who alone can strengthen you to bear the burdens of this world, the source of goodness, the spring from which right living flows, the fountain of all true fellowship? Do you believe that all this can come only from the Holy Ghost? Are you ready to depend on it with your life?

170

"Do you promise to abide in this Faith and in the covenant of your baptism, and as a member of the Church to be diligent in the use of the Means of Grace and in prayer?" This Christian faith, as you have learned to understand it through Lutheran teachers—will you let it mold your nature? Are you ready to go into life, wherever it takes you, whatever it brings, and bear all things, believe all right things, hope for all the things God desires, and endure everything as a faithful follower of Christ and a member of his church? 508°

These are the questions you will be asked. These are the questions you have to answer sincerely.

It is impossible to say "Of course" to any of those questions. No Christian could be that sure of himself. After all, we aren't saints; we're sinners. Are you sure you renounce? Are you sure you believe? Are you sure you promise to abide? Of course not. And that's why the last answer you give isn't a simple, "Yes." 509°

When Dr. Martin Luther stood before the assembly at Worms and had to say whether he would stick to his previous statements or back down, he answered, "Here I stand. I cannot do differently." Then he added, "God help me. Amen." When the early church leader, Augustine, was especially concerned about his faith, he prayed, "God, I believe: help my unbelief." If you want to be confirmed, you will answer those five questions by saying, "I do, *by the help of God.*"

God and the church know you are a sinner. There will be innumerable times when you renounce God instead of the devil; there will be innumerable times when you won't know what you believe; and there will be a seemingly endless succession of times when you are not faithful to the church. You are a sinner. You know it; God knows it; the church knows it. God knows you also are his adopted child. The church knows you also can be a saint. Believe this yourself. Trust in it, by the help of God. 510°

The choice before you is not whether you are going to be perfect or not. God forbid that this should ever be our choice.

The choice is whether you want to commit yourself to the Christian life or something else. The church is offering you the opportunity to be confirmed in your baptism covenant. You don't have to. You can be a Communist; you can be a follower of American capitalism; you can believe in man as God; and maybe you can even manage to believe in nothing. There are many, many different ways of life you can choose, many leaders eager to have you serve their cause. The only decision you have to make now is whether you accept God.

If you accept God, though, remember that he makes a tremendous demand, that he is exclusive: "I am the Lord thy God. Thou shalt have no other gods!" Take it or leave it.

511°　It's only fair to warn you again that Christianity is not "practical." For one thing, the church is asking you to become part of a fellowship often composed of social outcasts, misfits, oddballs, sinners, and what have you. In many parts of the world this fellowship is despised. This fellowship, which consists of eggheads, ignorant primitives, Caucasians, Negroes, Chinese —all sorts—this fellowship kneels beside you when you commune and when you pray. They'll all have personality defects. Some will be snobbish, some will be overbearing, some will be mean. You aren't expected merely to tolerate these humans; you are expected to love them. Each of them! All of them! Of course, they are expected to love you, too.

512　Another "impractical" thing asked of you is that you accept for yourself standards of living much higher than those by which the rest of the world operates. This puts you at a disadvantage. It's a disadvantage in the business world, the political world, the social world, and in your personal life, because you will be more critical of yourself.

513°　If you are a Christian, you will be out of step with the rest of the world. You'll be marching to a different drum beat, which others won't even hear. All the signs of success which you see around you, like financial wealth, power, prestige, possession of many material things, an adventurous sensual life, free and easy physical pleasure—things like these aren't likely

172

to be yours. You'll have something else, of course. But don't count on these other things, too.

It's only fair to warn you that Christianity isn't "practical." Look what happened to Jesus. They killed him. Look what happened to Christians in the early church. They tortured them. Look what's happening now.

A girl from an Orthodox Jewish family falls in love with a Christian boy. As she learns to know his religion she becomes more and more interested in Jesus. She decides to be a Christian herself. When she informs her family of this decision, she is expelled by her parents. She can never return home. They act as though she were dead. All her former friends ignore her. Her ties with the past are wiped out. She knew this might occur. She was ready. It was her choice. It doesn't always happen this way, but it does happen often, even today.

Or look what's happening to a native of Africa or Burma. He hears a Christian missionary. He is thrilled with the gospel. He becomes Christian. He also becomes an outcast of his society. His former way of life is gone. There is no Christian community to which he can go. He lives out his days in a lonely existence, occasionally seeing another Christian, otherwise by himself. He knew this might happen. He was ready. It was his choice. It doesn't always happen this way, but it does happen often, even today.

Or look at the teenage Christian in a communist country. His friends consider him behind the times. They are afraid to associate with him. Pressures are put on him to join the Party. His education is threatened. There will be no college for him if he remains a Christian, no good jobs, no respect by the young people around him. He, too, knew this might happen. It was his choice to be confirmed as a Christian. He chose willingly. It doesn't always happen this way, but often.

Don't assume that you, if you choose to be confirmed, will 514° necessarily escape a similar future. In America ordinary church members are acceptable. The really faithful Christian may find himself thought to be a bit odd, but tolerated. What tomorrow

173

will bring only God knows. It's not likely that you will have to give your life as a result of your choice to be Christian, but it's possible. It's happened before. It is happening elsewhere. It will happen again. It's only fair to warn you.

515   If Christianity isn't practical, then why do people become Christians? Because they believe that Jesus Christ is the Way, the Truth, and the Life. Perhaps the Christian life is impractical on this earth, at this time, in this society. But God rules the universe, for all time, and is the source of all society, all fellowship, all life.

If a fellow actor tells you how to do your part in a play, but the director has other ideas, whom do you follow? The director, naturally, because he sees the whole thing and knows how the play needs to turn out.

The prophet Amos once said, "If a lion roars, who does not tremble? If God speaks, who does not listen?"

516*   If you decide to be confirmed in your Christian faith, it should not be for the hope of glory or reward. Even if there were no heaven to gain or hell to flee, for what God is you should love him. God so loved the world that he gave *you* his only Son. Be faithful to him, and you will not perish. The church will state firmly (confirm) that you are in the faithful
517   remnant. The Father in heaven, for Jesus' sake, will renew and increase in you the gift of the Holy Ghost, to your strengthening in faith, to your growth in grace, to your patience in suffering, and to the blessed hope of everlasting life.

518
519*   God puts no pressure on you to accept him. As far as he is concerned, your choice is free. Further, he is patient; if you are alive tomorrow or the day after, the choice will still be there. If you don't want to be a Christian, for heaven's sake, and for yours too, don't pretend to be one.

We Christians believe that the Christian life is the only real
520*   life there is. We know you were baptized into our family. The church is ready to confirm your relationship to it and to God. Whether you are confirmed or not, God will always love you.

You are called to be Christian. This is the word of God.

174

The Small Catechism

THE TEN COMMANDMENTS

The First Commandment

I am the Lord thy God. Thou shalt have no other gods before me.

(Thou shalt not make unto thee any graven image or any likeness of anything that is in the heaven above, or that is in the earth beneath, or that is in the water under the earth; thou shalt not bow down thyself to them, nor serve them; for I the Lord thy God am a jealous God, visiting the iniquity of the fathers upon the children unto the third and fourth generation of them that hate me; and showing mercy unto thousands of them that love me, and keep my commandments.)

What is meant by this Commandment?

We should fear, love, and trust in God above all things.

The Second Commandment

Thou shalt not take the name of the Lord they God in vain; for the Lord will not hold him guiltless that taketh his name in vain.

What is meant by this Commandment?

We should so fear and love God as not to curse, swear, conjure, lie, or deceive, by his name, but call upon him in every time of need, and worship him with prayer, praise and thanksgiving.

The Third Commandment

Remember the Sabbath-day, to keep it holy.

(Six days shalt thou labor, and do all thy work; but the seventh day is the Sabbath of the Lord thy God: in it thou shalt not do any work, thou, nor thy son, nor thy daughter, nor thy man-servant, nor thy maid-servant, nor thy cattle, nor thy stranger that is within thy gates: for in six days the Lord made heaven and earth, the sea, and all that in them is, and rested the seventh day; wherefore the Lord blessed the Sabbath-day, and hallowed it.)

What is meant by this Commandment?

We should so fear and love God as not to despise his Word and the preaching of the Gospel, but deem it holy, and willingly hear and learn it.

The Fourth Commandment

Honor thy father and thy mother, that thy days may be long upon the land which the Lord thy God giveth thee.

What is meant by this Commandment?

We should so fear and love God as not to despise nor displease our parents and superiors, but honor, serve, obey, love, and esteem them.

The Fifth Commandment

Thou shalt not kill.

What is meant by this Commandment?

We should so fear and love God as not to do our neighbor any bodily harm or injury, but rather assist and comfort him in danger and want.

The Sixth Commandment

Thou shalt not commit adultery.

What is meant by this Commandment?

We should so fear and love God as to be chaste and pure in our words and deeds, each one also loving and honoring his wife or her husband.

The Seventh Commandment

Thou shalt not steal.

What is meant by this Commandment?

We should so fear and love God as not to rob our neighbor of his money or property, nor bring it into our possession by unfair dealing or fraudulent means, but rather assist him to improve and protect it.

The Eighth Commandment

Thou shalt not bear false witness against thy neighbor.

What is meant by this Commandment?

We should so fear and love God as not deceitfully to belie, betray, slander, nor raise injurious reports against our neighbor, but apologize for him, speak well of him, and put the most charitable construction on all his actions.

The Ninth Commandment

Thou shalt not covet thy neighbor's house.

What is meant by this Commandment?

We should so fear and love God as not to desire by craftiness to gain possession of our neighbor's inheritance or home, or to obtain it under the pretext of a legal right, but be ready to assist and serve him in the preservation of his own.

The Tenth Commandment

Thou shalt not covet thy neighbor's wife, nor his man-servant, nor his maid-servant, nor his ox, nor his ass, nor anything that is thy neighbor's.

What is meant by this Commandment?

We should so fear and love God as not to alienate our neighbor's wife from him, entice away his servants, nor let loose his cattle, but use our endeavors that they may remain and discharge their duty to him.

What does God declare concerning all these Commandments?

He says: I the Lord thy God am a jealous God, visiting the iniquity of the fathers upon the children unto the third and fourth generation of them that hate me; and showing mercy unto thousands of them that love me and keep my commandments.

What is meant by this declaration?

God threatens to punish all those who transgress these commandments. We should, therefore, dread his displeasure, and not act contrarily to these commandments. But he promises grace and every blessing to all who keep them. We should, therefore, love and trust in him, and cheerfully do what he has commanded us.

THE CREED

First Article—of Creation

I believe in God the Father Almighty, Maker of heaven and earth.

What is meant by this Article?

I believe that God has created me and all that exists; that he has given and still preserves to me my body and soul with all my limbs and senses, my reason and all the faculties of my mind, together with my raiment, food, home, and family, and all my property; that he daily provides me abundantly with all the necessaries of life, protects me from all danger, and preserves me and guards me against all evil; all which he does out of pure, paternal, and divine goodness and mercy, without any merit or worthiness in me; for all which I am in duty bound to thank, praise, serve, and obey him. This is most certainly true.

Second Article—of Redemption

And in Jesus Christ, his only Son, our Lord; who was conceived by the Holy Ghost, born of the Virgin Mary; suffered under Pontius Pilate, was crucified, dead, and buried; he descended into hell; the third day he rose again from the dead; he ascended into heaven, and sitteth on the right hand of God the Father Almighty; from thence he shall come to judge the quick and the dead.

What is meant by this Article?

I believe that Jesus Christ, true God, begotten of the Father from eternity, and also true man, born of the Virgin Mary, is my Lord; who has redeemed me, a lost and condemned creature, secured and delivered me from all sins, from death, and from the power of the devil; not with silver and gold, but with his holy and precious blood, and with his innocent sufferings and death; in order that I might be his, live under him in his kingdom, and serve him in everlasting righteousness, innocence, and blessedness; even as he is risen from the dead, and lives and reigns to all eternity. This is most certainly true.

Third Article—of Sanctification

I believe in the Holy Ghost; the holy Christian church, the communion of saints; the forgiveness of sins; the resurrection of the body; and the life everlasting. Amen.

What is meant by this Article?

I believe that I cannot by my own reason or strength believe in Jesus Christ my Lord, or come to him; but the Holy Ghost has called me through the Gospel, enlightened me by his gifts, and sanctified and preserved me in the true faith; in like manner as he calls, gathers, enlightens, and sanctifies the whole Christian church on earth, and preserves it in union with Jesus Christ in the true faith; in which Christian church he daily forgives abundantly all my sins, and the sins of all believers, and will raise up me and all the dead at the last day, and will grant everlasting life to me and to all who believe in Christ. This is most certainly true.

THE LORD'S PRAYER

Introduction

Our Father who art in heaven

What is meant by this Introduction?

God would thereby affectionately encourage us to believe that he is truly our Father, and that we are his children indeed, so that we may call upon him with all cheerfulness and confidence, even as beloved children entreat their affectionate parent.

First Petition

Hallowed be thy name.

What is meant by this Petition?

The name of God is indeed holy in itself, but we pray in this petition that it may be hallowed also by us.

178

How is this effected?

When the Word of God is taught in its truth and purity, and we, as the children of God, lead holy lives, in accordance with it; to this may our blessed Father in heaven help us! But whoever teaches and lives otherwise than as God's Word prescribes, profanes the name of God among us; from this preserve us, heavenly Father!

Second Petition

Thy Kingdom come.

What is meant by this Petition?

The kingdom of God comes indeed of itself, without our prayers; but we pray in this petition that it may come unto us also.

When is this effected?

When our heavenly Father gives us his Holy Spirit, so that by his grace we believe his holy Word, and live a godly life here on earth, and in heaven forever.

Third Petition

Thy will be done on earth, as it is in heaven

What is meant by this Petition?

The good and gracious will of God is done indeed without our prayer; but we pray in this petition that it may be done by us also.

When is this effected?

When God frustrates and brings to naught every evil counsel and purpose, which would hinder us from hallowing the name of God, and prevent his kingdom from coming to us, such as the will of the devil, of the world, and of our own flesh; and when he strengthens us, and keeps us steadfast in his Word, and in the faith, even unto our end. This is his gracious and good will.

Fourth Petition

Give us this day our daily bread.

What is meant by this Petition?

God gives indeed without our prayer even to the wicked also their daily bread; but we pray in this petition that he would make us sensible of his benefits, and enable us to receive our daily bread with thanksgiving.

What is implied in the word, "our daily bread"?

All things that pertain to the wants and the support of this present life; such as food, raiment, money, goods, house and land, and other property; a believing spouse and good children; trustworthy servants

179

and faithful magistrates; favorable seasons, peace and health; education and honor; true friends, good neighbors, and the like.

Fifth Petition

And forgive us our trespasses, as we forgive those who trespass against us.

What is meant by this Petition?

We pray in this petition that our heavenly Father would not regard our sins, nor deny us our requests on account of them; for we are not worthy of anything for which we pray, and have not merited it; but that he would grant us all things through grace, although we daily commit much sin, and deserve chastisement alone. We will therefore, on our part, both heartily forgive, and also readily do good to those who may injure or offend us.

Sixth Petition

And lead us not into temptation.

What is meant by this Petition?

God indeed tempts no one to sin; but we pray in this petition that God would so guard and preserve us, that the devil, the world, and our own flesh, may not deceive us, nor lead us into error and unbelief, despair, and other great and shameful sins; and that, though we may be thus tempted, we may, nevertheless, finally prevail and gain the victory.

Seventh Petition

But deliver us from evil.

What is meant by this Petition?

We pray in this petition, as in a summary, that our heavenly Father would deliver us from all manner of evil, whether it affect the body or soul, property or character, and at last, when the hour of death shall arrive, grant us a happy end, and graciously take us from this world of sorrow to himself in heaven.

Conclusion

For thine is the kingdom, and the power, and the glory, for ever and ever.   Amen.

What is meant by the word "Amen"?

That I should be assured that such petitions are acceptable to our heavenly Father, and are heard by him; for he himself has commanded us to pray in this manner, and has promised that he will hear us. Amen, amen, that is, yea, yea, it shall be so.

180

THE SACRAMENT OF HOLY BAPTISM

I. What is Baptism?

Baptism is not simply water, but it is the water comprehended in God's command, and connected with God's Word.

What is that Word of God?

It is that which our Lord Jesus Christ spoke, as it is recorded in the last chapter of Matthew, verse 19: "Go ye, and teach all nations, baptizing them in the name of the Father, and of the Son, and of the Holy Ghost."

II. What gifts or benefits does baptism confer?

It works forgiveness of sins, delivers from death and the devil, and confers everlasting salvation on all who believe, as the Word and promise of God declare.

What are such words and promises of God?

Those which our Lord Jesus Christ spoke, as they are recorded in the last chapter of Mark, verse 16: "He that believeth and is baptized, shall be saved; but he that believeth not shall be damned."

III. How can water produce such great effects?

It is not the water indeed that produces these effects, but the Word of God which accompanies and is connected with the water, and our faith, which relies on the Word of God connected with the water. For the water, without the Word of God, is simply water and no baptism. But when connected with the Word of God, it is a baptism, that is, a gracious water of life, and a "washing of regeneration" in the Holy Ghost; as St. Paul says to Titus, in the third chapter, verses 5-8: "According to his mercy he saved us, by the washing of regeneration, and renewing of the Holy Ghost; which he shed on us abundantly through Jesus Christ our Saviour; that being justified by his grace, we should be made heirs according to the hope of eternal life. This is a faithful saying."

IV. What does such baptizing with water signify?

It signifies that the old Adam in us is to be drowned and destroyed by daily sorrow and repentance, together with all sins and evil lusts; and that again the new man should daily come forth and rise, that shall live in the presence of God in righteousness and purity forever.

Where is it so written?

St. Paul, in the Epistle to the Romans, chapter 6, verse 4, says: "We are buried with Christ by baptism into death; that like as he was raised up from the dead by the glory of the Father, even so we also should walk in newness of life."

181

THE SACRAMENT OF THE ALTAR

What is the Sacrament of the Altar?

It is the true body and blood of our Lord Jesus Christ, under the bread and wine, given unto us Christians to eat and to drink, as it was instituted by Christ himself.

Where is it so written?

The holy Evangelists, Matthew, Mark, and Luke, together with St. Paul, write thus:

"Our Lord Jesus Christ, the same night in which he was betrayed, took bread: and when he had given thanks, he brake it, and gave it to his disciples, and said, Take, eat; this is my body, which is given for you: this do, in remembrance of me.

"After the same manner also he took the cup, when he had supped, gave thanks, and gave it to them, saying, Drink ye all of it; this cup is the new testament in my blood, which is shed for you, for the remission of sins; this do, as oft as ye drink it, in remembrance of me."

What benefits are derived from such eating and drinking?

They are pointed out in these words: "given and shed for you, for the remission of sins." Namely, through these words, the remission of sins, life and salvation are granted unto us in the Sacrament. For where there is remission of sins, there are also life and salvation.

How can the bodily eating and drinking produce such great effects?

The eating and the drinking, indeed, do not produce them, but the words which stand here, namely: "given and shed for you, for the remission of sins." These words are, besides the bodily eating and drinking, the chief things in the Sacrament: and he who believes these words, has that which they declare and set forth, namely, the remission of sins.

Who is it, then, that receives this Sacrament worthily?

Fasting and bodily preparation are indeed a good external discipline; but he is truly worthy and well prepared who believes these words, "given and shed for you, for the remission of sins." But he who does not believe these words, or who doubts, is unworthy and unfit; for the words: "for you," require truly-believing hearts.

Index I

184

Index II

When hymn numbers are followed by a dash and another number, that indicates the number of the stanza that is applicable. For instance, 456-2 refers to the second stanza of hymn 456. Items listed may refer to only one thought or several in a paragraph.

The Bible passages listed in this index show that many of the ideas contained in this book are similar to ideas held by writers of Scripture. The passages are not intended to prove an idea, or even necessarily to show from where it was drawn. The Christian faith does not grow out of a collection of Bible passages, but out of a personal relationship with Jesus Christ, made possible by the Word of God revealed in the whole of Scripture.

Margin Number	Bible Passage	Hymn in Service Book and Hymnal
1		449
2	Jer. 10:12 Ps. 104:24 Rom. 11:33, 34	322-3 354-4
3	Ps. 139:1-6	484
4	Jn. 14:6	390
5		356-1
6	Is. 40:28 1 Cor. 2:10, 11	454
8	Ps. 139:1-12	322-1
10	Ps. 102:24-27 2 Peter 3:8	
12	Ecc. 3:11	161-5 168 287-4
17	Job 11:7, 9	354-3 9
18	Job 42:1-3 Is. 55:8, 9 Is. 6:3 Is. 5:16	181-1, 2, 3 468-1 484
19		484-6 582-2
20	Gen. 1:27-31 Gen. 3:1-8	
21	Rom. 5:12	
22	Ps. 10:4 2 Cor. 1:9	
23	John 1:1-4 John 5:39	
24	John 1:14	252
27	Ps. 3:4-7 Is. 40:8	
28	Is. 55:10, 11 Jer. 23:29 Luke 8:4-15	254-2
30	1 Cor. 15:10 Rom. 11:6	
35	Gen. 3:8 Ex. 19:16-25 1 Sam. 3 Acts 9:1-10	

182	1 Chron. 16:29 Jn. 4:23, 24	389-1 451-3, **4**
	Acts 17:24, 25	
184	Ps. 95:6	227-3
185	1 Thess. 5:17, **18**	458
186	Col. 4:2	
187	Heb. 4:16	
188	Phil. 4:**6**	
189	Eph. 6:18 1 Tim. 2:**1, 2**	
191	Mt. 6:9-13 Luke 11:1-4	452-1
193	Mt. 7:11 Rom. 8:15	
194	Jn. 17:6 Mk. 1:14, 15	318 331-1, 2 **465**
	Rom. 8:28	
196	1 Tim. 6:6-8 Mt. 6:31-**33**	
197	Ps. 32:5	
198	Mt. 6:14, 15	
199	Mt. 26:41 Mk. 4:1-20	
	Eph. 6:11 Jas. 1:13-15	
200	Ps. 34:15-19	
203	Mt. 7:7, 8 Jn. 16:23-27	
208		**579-5**
210	1 John 5:14	459
212	Eph. 2:18	
219	Titus 2:14 Col. 1:10	379-2, 3 **385-1**
220	Luke 6:43-45	
221	Heb. 2:4 Rom. 3:28	193-2
222		493-8
225	Jas. 2:10	
226	2 Chron. 7:14 Is. 55:**7**	366-2
227	Mt. 4:17 Jas. 4:8-10	
228		379-3
230	I Thess. 5:23	
231		397-4
232	1 Cor. 15:22	
233	Gal. 2:20 Luke 17:20, **21**	
234	Rom. 8:31-39	68 **166-1**
235	Mt. 12:31	
236	Jn. 3:1-5	397-4
237	Is. 14:12-15	
239	1 Cor. 15:56, **57**	
240	2 Cor. 5:16, **17**	150-4 558-5
243	Rom. 12:2	
244		290-3
245	2 Kings 6:11-**17**	

188

331	Is. 40:1-26; 44:6 Mt. 4:10	466-5			
332	Mt. 5:34-37 Lev. 19:12				
	Mt. 12:36				
333	Gen. 2:1-3 Ex. 20:8-11				
334	Luke 6:1-5 Mt. 28:1				
	Heb. 10:23-25				
335	Rom. 13:1				
336	Mt. 5:44, 45 Mt. 5:21, 22				
	Eph. 4:31, 32				
337	1 Cor. 3:16, 17 Mt. 19:6	301-2			
338	Eph. 4:28 Mt. 7:12				
339	Eph. 4:25 Mt. 7:1, 2				
	Ps. 34:13				
340	Luke 12:15 Phil. 2:3, 4				
343	Mt. 28:18-20	544-4			
344	Mark 1:32-34	351	232-1		
347	Mt. 25:31-46				
348	1 Kings 22:14				
349		217			
353	Jer. 26:2 Amos 3:7, 8	340-1	345-2		
356	Jer. 1:4-10 Is. 8:11, 12	341-2			
358	Acts 6:8; 7:2a, 51-60				
362	Luke 10:1-9	310	316-5		
363	Acts 10:42 Jas. 5:19, 20	250-4	306-5	307	
364	Rom. 10:13-17				
365	Rev. 1:6 Mt. 27:50, 51	401-2			
366	Ez. 33:1-9	255-1	161		
367	Gen. 1:27-31 1 Tim. 4:4, 5	339-4	347-1		
	Ps. 19:1 2 Cor. 6:16				
368	Gen. 1 Is. 45:18, 19				
369	1 Cor. 4:1, 2 1 Pet. 4:8-11	544-2			
371	Rom. 8:28 Acts 13:52	213-4			
372	Heb. 11:13-16 1 John 3:1	487-1	520	529	165-3
	Luke 12:32-34 2 Cor. 5:1-9				
373	2 Kings 19:29-31 Is. 7:3				
	Is. 10:20-23				
374	Rom. 11:1-6				
379	Col. 1:17-20 Eph. 2:19-22	149-1	242-1		
383	Ps. 122:1				
384		539-1			
385	Mk. 7:1-9				
386	1 Cor. 14:26-40 Eph. 4:11-15				
	1 Tim. 3:1-13 1 Tim. 4:6-16				

190

387	1 Cor. 3:1-9	
390		153-4
393	Mt. 18:20 Ps. 27:4-6	187 543-2
394		239
396	Ps. 150 Ps. 149:1-4	
397	Num. 6:22-27 2 Cor. 13:14	
402	1 Cor. 11:23-26	
406	Mt. 28:19 1 Cor. 11:25	
407	Acts 2:38 Mt. 26:28	
409	John 3:5 Acts 10:47, 48 Mt. 26:26, 27	275-2
413	Mt. 2:4-17	
414	Mk. 1:9, 10	
415	Acts 16:33, 34 1 Cor. 1:16	336-3
416		335-5
417		260-3
420	Acts 22:16 1 Cor. 10:1-4	
421	Rom. 6:3, 4 John 15:1-6 Gal. 3:26, 27	259-1
422		489-1 493-5
424	Ex. 12:21-24	
425	1 Cor. 11:23-25 Mt. 26:28	266
427	John 6:56 1 Cor. 10:16 1 Cor. 11:29	
428	Mt. 26:29 John 14:18-23	263-1 265-1 271-3 164 267-1
429	1 Cor. 10:17 1 Cor. 12:13 Rom. 12:5	282-3
430		143-3 149-4
436	1 Cor. 11:17-33	273-5 149-2
442	Acts 11:26 1 Pet. 4:16, 17	
445	2 Cor. 11:1, 12:13	
450		149-2
451		157-4
452	Eph. 4:15, 16	
453	1 Tim. 4:1-4	
458	Ps. 35:1-3 Eph. 6:10-17 Mt. 5:1-11 2 Tim. 2:1-10 2 Tim. 4:6, 7 Heb. 11:1; 12:4, 12	149 308-2, 3 68 554 560 564 567 562 532-1 154-1
459		158 144
460	Heb. 11:13-16 Heb. 12:22-24 Rev. 7:9-17	273-8 296-2, 4 600-1, 2 595-1

Type used in this book
Body, 10 on 13 Caledonia
Display, Tempo
Paper: "R" Standard White Antique